ACQUISITION STRATEGIES *for* ESOP COMPANIES

Fourth Edition

John Burgess • Lynn DuBois • Daniel Goldstein • Mary Josephs
Dustin Kim • William W. Merten • Corey Rosen • John Solimine
Carter Wideman

The National Center for Employee Ownership
Visit us at **www.nceo.org** for more information about ESOPs

This publication is designed to provide accurate and authoritative information in regard to the subject matter covered. It is sold with the understanding that the publisher is not engaged in rendering legal, accounting, or other professional service. If legal advice or other expert assistance is required, the services of a competent professional person should be sought.

Legal, accounting, and other rules affecting business often change. Before making decisions based on the information you find here or in any publication from any publisher, you should ascertain what changes might have occurred and what changes might be forthcoming. The NCEO's website (including the members-only resources) and newsletter for members provide regular updates on these changes. If you have any questions or concerns about a particular issue, check with your professional advisor or, if you are an NCEO member, call or email us.

Acquisition Strategies for ESOP Companies, 4th Ed.

John Burgess, Lynn DuBois, Daniel Goldstein, Mary Josephs, Dustin Kim, William W. Merten, Corey Rosen, John Solimine, and Carter Wideman

Book design by Scott Rodrick

ISBN: 978-1-954990-66-1

The National Center for Employee Ownership
Phone: (510) 208-1300
Website: www.nceo.org

Contents

Introduction 1
Corey Rosen
About the Fourth Edition **2**

1. Preparing for an Acquisition 3
Mary Josephs and Carter Wideman
Defining and Determining Value **4**
Building Growth Versus Buying Growth with Acquisitions **5**
Common Valuation Methodologies for M&A Acquisition Targets **6**
Developing a Strategy for a Disciplined Acquisition Process **8**
"Cleaning the House": What Makes an Attractive Buyer **11**
Identifying the Right Supporting Cast for Acquisitions **14**
What's Your Capacity? Debt and Leadership **16**
The M&A Process from Start to Finish **17**
Considerations for ESOP Companies and ESOP-to-ESOP Mergers **20**
Conclusion **22**

2. Managing Risk 23
Lynn DuBois
Due Diligence and the Purchase Agreement **23**
Fiduciary Issues for the Board of Directors **35**
Issues for Trustees to Consider **37**

3. Using ESOPs in Mergers and Acquisitions 41
William W. Merten
General Planning Considerations **41**
When Section 1042 Treatment Is Desired by Target Shareholders **47**

When Section 1042 Treatment Is Not Desired by Target Shareholders **52**
Acquisition Fiduciary and Settlor Issues **56**
Acquisition Corporate Governance Issues **56**
Acquisition Financing Concerns **57**
Conclusion **58**

4. Should a Company Acquire or Merge with an ESOP Company? 59
John Burgess
Asset Acquisitions **60**
Stock Acquisitions **62**
Mergers **63**

5. Issues for ESOP Companies Acquiring Other ESOP Companies 65
Corey Rosen
Factors That Cause Mergers to Succeed or Fail **66**
Valuation of the Combined Entities **69**
Protecting the Interests of Each Company's ESOP **71**
Reconciling Plan Differences **73**
Other Employee Benefits and Compensation **75**
Combining a Mature ESOP with a Young ESOP **75**
Communicating the Transaction **77**
Appendix: Survey Questions for Key Participants to Assess Mergers and Acquisitions **78**

6. A Step-by-Step Guide to Pursuing Acquisitions 81
Corey Rosen
A Roadmap for Approaching Acquisitions **83**
Appendix: Further Resources **89**

7. M&A Strategy: The Essential Steps to Growing ESOP Companies Through Acquisitions 91
Mary Josephs and Dustin Kim
The ESOP Advantage in Acquisitions **91**
Why Create an M&A Strategy? **92**

Conduct a Self-Assessment **93**
Developing Your Acquisition Strategy **94**
How to Execute the Strategy **101**
Integration: The Key Often-Missed Step **105**
Conclusion **106**

8. ESOP Company Acquisition Case Studies 107
Mary Josephs, Dustin Kim, Corey Rosen, and Carter Wideman
Border States **107**
HB Global **110**
Hypertherm **112**
Jasper Holdings **115**
Proponent **117**
Empowered Ventures **119**
Roush Auto Group **122**

9. Financing Alternatives for ESOPs Pursuing M&A 125
John Solimine
Commercial Bank Debt: Revolving Credit Facilities or Term Loan **125**
Nonbank Debt: Term Loan or Unitranche Facilities **127**
Mezzanine Debt **128**
Structured or Minority Equity via Drop-Down LLC **129**

10. Should You Create a Holding Company? 131
Daniel Goldstein
What Is a Holding Company? **131**
Acquisitions and Brand Identity, with a Few Miscellaneous Considerations **132**
Administrative Decisions: Complexity and Flexibility **134**
Culture and Synergies **136**
It Depends... **137**

About the Authors 139

About the NCEO 143

Introduction

Corey Rosen

THIS BOOK provides a practical, detailed guide to making acquisitions in ESOP companies. Such companies have been extremely active in the merger and acquisition market in recent years. For instance, in 2021, more than 400,000 new participants were added to ESOP companies, about 70% of whom came from acquisitions by ESOP companies of other companies. There are many reasons for this, but the most important is that after ESOP companies have paid off their acquisition debt, they often accumulate significant cash and strength in the market, both through the performance improvements attributable to the ESOP as well as not having to fund federal and state income tax bills if the company is a 100% ESOP-owned S corporation.

Selling to an ESOP can be very appealing for company owners seeking a business transition. As discussed in the case study chapter of this book, selling owners and top executives often talk about how much they value the idea that the ESOP company making the acquisition will make everyone an owner, frequently while maintaining current management and even the autonomy of the business unit. They also note that ESOP companies have an outstanding track record of maintaining employment at the target company; this stands in sharp contrast to the experience of sales to private equity firms, which have a very mixed record on maintaining employment in the companies that they buy. Sellers to an ESOP get a fair price and can feel good about the legacy that they are creating.

In a 2015 study by Suzanne Cromlish, then at Case Western Reserve University, of 467 ESOP company acquisitions by 87 ESOP companies, 442 were considered successful by the acquiring company. All but five of the acquiring companies retained 90% to 100% of the employees in all of their acquisitions. This is much better performance than has been the case for mergers and acquisitions in general.

Structuring acquisitions in ESOP companies can be done in various ways, from relatively straightforward deals to more complex transactions that allow the seller to defer tax on the gain from the sale to the ESOP company. ESOP acquisitions also involve potential fiduciary issues and, like all acquisitions, require a dedicated integration team. Because ESOP cultures tend to be distinctive, it is also critical that the integration process pays particular attention to cultural integration.

We appreciate the contributions of the authors of this book and would be interested in any comments you might have; email feedback to customerservice@nceo.org.

About the Fourth Edition

For the fourth edition (2026), the existing chapters were reviewed and updated or replaced where needed. Chapter 1 was completely rewritten; chapter 2 did not need any changes; the chapter on making an acquisition successful was replaced by a step-by-step guide to acquisitions; and the other existing chapters were updated. We also added a new chapter on whether a company should acquire or merge with an ESOP company, and added three new case studies to the case study chapter.

CHAPTER 1

Preparing for an Acquisition

Mary Josephs and Carter Wideman

VALUE CREATION is a fundamental part of business strategy, and the underlying premise is that a company's value increases when it can generate greater future cash flows, reduce the risk associated with those cash flows, or both. Acquisitions can be an effective tool for achieving these outcomes in a management team's value-creation plan. However, they are among the most labor-intensive forms of corporate growth, often requiring significant company resources to complete. To that end, preparedness is often the differentiator between successful and unsuccessful acquisitions, and a proper strategy helps achieve an efficient, disciplined process.

This chapter covers the following topics to provide a framework for understanding the key components of valuation, acquisition readiness, and the M&A process that are intertwined when designing a strategy for growth through acquisitions:

- Defining and determining value
- Building growth versus buying growth with acquisitions

This chapter is an update and expansion of the chapter "Acquisitions as Part of Business Strategy" from previous editions of this publication, originally written by the late John Miscione.

- Common valuation methodologies for M&A acquisition targets
- Developing a disciplined acquisition process
- What makes an attractive buyer
- Choosing the right team for acquisitions
- Debt capacity and leadership capacity
- The M&A process from start to finish
- Considerations for ESOP companies and ESOP-to-ESOP mergers

Defining and Determining Value

The value of a business is its enterprise value, which reflects the aggregate value of a company's operating business, inclusive of both debt and equity capital. If management can grow enterprise value, equity value (the value available to all equity holders after all claims are satisfied) should grow as well. Before taking into consideration third-party claims on valuation, the value of the company's operating assets can be estimated as a function of two things: the cash flows the assets generate and the enterprise (EBITDA) multiple applied to those cash flows:

Enterprise Value = EBITDA x Enterprise (EBITDA) Multiple

A common proxy for a company's cash flows is EBITDA (earnings before interest, taxes, depreciation, and amortization). EBITDA represents what remains after all cash expenses are deducted from a company's revenues. The enterprise multiple is a multidimensional valuation factor derived from several parameters, some of which are within a company's control and others that are not. Factors outside the company's control are determined by financial markets and the industry in which the company operates. Therefore, enterprise multiples vary by company and by industry.

The most controllable input in the enterprise multiple is the company's EBITDA growth rate. Controlling for all other factors, the faster a company's EBITDA grows compared to others in its industry, the more likely potential buyers will pay a premium to acquire the business. The impact of the EBITDA growth rate on a company's enterprise multiple can be even more pronounced if that growth can be sustained over extended periods. Other controllable inputs include superior margins compared to industry benchmarks, revenue visibility, customer diversification, and sustainable competitive advantages, among others.

What makes acquisitions an attractive growth strategy for many companies is that many of these inputs can be achieved through mergers, especially if the company has exhausted its organic strategies. Each of these factors is assessed not only when determining the target's value but also when evaluating the company's internal value. This sets expectations for the amount of capital financing that is achievable for a transaction and, with that, the valuation range for targets that the company has the capacity to acquire.

Building Growth Versus Buying Growth with Acquisitions

Before a company can make an informed decision about committing to finding targets and making acquisitions, its management team must be confident that this is the best growth strategy at this stage of the company's life cycle. For this discussion, we will focus on how a company can grow its EBITDA. At a high level, it can achieve this in two ways: (1) increasing revenues and (2) reducing costs. When a company increases revenues faster than its cost of goods sold (COGS), it creates an incremental gross margin. If the operating expenses (OPEX) do not exceed that incremental gross margin, a significant portion of that gross profit will be added to EBITDA. The ability to increase revenue is limited by both the size of the market the company competes in and the number of competitors. Companies can cut costs by increasing the efficiency of production (reducing COGS) and/or administration (reducing OPEX)—in short, doing more with less. However, cutting costs can also reduce overall production or the quality of offerings, so these decisions need to be weighed carefully.

Revenue increases and cost reductions can be achieved through investments in new initiatives by the existing business (building growth) or through an acquisition strategy (buying growth). Both approaches have pros and cons that need to be considered. An advantage of a build strategy is that it allows a company to keep complete control over the new business initiative. Moreover, the business grows within the bounds of its existing management processes, financial and information systems, and, most importantly, culture. This eliminates the need for integration processes required when employing a buy strategy.

On the other hand, build strategies generally take longer to generate cash flow. Think of the time it takes to develop market share when introducing a product to a new market. It can take months, even years, to achieve sustainable demand in a market where there is no established or understood demand for the offering, or where demand exists but other competitors already meet it. A second limitation of building is corporate management skills and/or technological know-how. Build strategies may require acquiring new employees or managers with different skill sets. It may also require acquiring technical know-how that does not currently exist within the company. For these reasons, in many circumstances, an acquisition strategy can be more effective.

The major difference in a buy strategy is that the company acquires the existing cash flow generated by an established business infrastructure. Consequently, with an acquisition strategy, a company may achieve faster growth. Additionally, it can quickly adopt new technology or human resources that it might otherwise not be able to develop internally. However, an acquisition is riskier. The company may not be able to generate sufficient cash flows to justify the price it paid. This is why a comprehensive due diligence and risk management process is necessary when using this strategy. Acquired companies often have different management, accounting, and information systems. In addition, there may be major cultural differences in the workforce that are difficult to overcome. These considerations must be evaluated to determine which kind of strategy makes the most sense for the buyer.

Common Valuation Methodologies for M&A Acquisition Targets

The valuation process used to determine a range of offer prices for a target is similar to that used to value an ESOP company's common stock. The process takes into consideration both historical and projected financial data. The data is then used to calculate a range of values for the target. In general, three methodologies are used: (1) the comparable public companies analysis, (2) the precedent M&A transaction analysis, and (3) the discounted cash flow analysis.

With the comparable public company analysis, values are calculated by applying valuation multiples derived from a sample of similar public companies to the target; most often, the companies are comparable by industry, offerings, end markets, and margins. With the precedent M&A transaction analysis, acquisition transactions involving similar companies are evaluated, and purchase price multiples from those transactions are applied to the target. With the discounted cash flow methodology, the target's projected future cash flows are discounted to present value using an appropriate discount rate and then combined with the terminal value's present value, which is discounted using the same rate. When used in tandem, these approaches provide three estimates of value that define a range within which the buyer should negotiate. At the same time, the target will have prepared its own calculations and valuation range to negotiate from. When considering the price to offer, the buyer must consider what the seller's range might be, as well as what price the target's board may require for a fairness opinion and transaction sign-off. This valuation exercise is highly dependent on the results of the financial due diligence process, as the acquirer must validate that the cash flows supporting the valuation are as described by the target.

Ultimately, there is no single price for an asset. The value of an asset lies within a range, and the final price is determined by negotiation. The result is a function of the strength of the buyer and the seller, in addition to the attractiveness of the asset. A desirable asset may be bought cheaply if the seller must sell. Conversely, a desirable asset in the hands of a seller with no compulsion to sell will command a higher price. The buyer must understand the asset's strategic value, alternative ways to acquire that value, and the downside risk of proceeding if the price is approaching the high end of its range. Critical to making the final offer is the buyer's financial strength. This strength is a function of its excess cash, its debt capacity, and, if necessary, its access to minority equity capital, all of which are discussed further later in the chapter.

Once a prospective buyer aligns on the value of its business and the methodologies that are employed to value targets, the foundation is set to begin defining an acquisition strategy.

Developing a Strategy for a Disciplined Acquisition Process

A detailed acquisition strategy is essential for identifying opportunities that create long-term value for the buyer. However, they are not developed overnight and are often a part of a company's multi-year planning process. The management team of a company should have a one-, three-, and/or five-year financial plan that details the expected financial performance of the company's lines of business. The plan should be developed by the leaders of the lines of business and should take into consideration the demand for each line of business's products or services, the competitive position of the business in its markets, and the resources required to increase market share or maintain the business's share of a growing market.

This plan, upon review by the board, sets out the objectives that the management team will manage toward, sets targets that will trigger bonuses, and, most importantly, projects the amount of cash the business will generate to maintain its capital plant, fund incremental working capital, pay dividends and/or redeem shares, and pay down debt and/or increase cash on hand. This plan lays out the baseline for value creation over the next five years. The review of this plan among the executive team and between the CEO and the board is the basis for considering an acquisition strategy as a potential approach for growing EBITDA and thus creating more value.

Moreover, the appropriateness of an acquisition strategy depends on the assessment of the financial plan. No two businesses are ever in the same place. Financial plans vary by company and reflect the state of the markets a company serves, the stage of development of the company, and the competitive position of the company. The plan may show a rapidly growing business with expanding markets and the necessary capacity to produce goods and services to develop incremental revenues and EBITDA. A business with this type of plan is not likely to need an acquisition strategy to grow. This is a build-from-within business.

On the other hand, the plan can show a mature business with limited growth opportunities for the company's revenues. This type of business may likely have modest investment needs, excess annual cash flow, high debt capacity, and perhaps even cash on hand in excess of day-to-day operating needs. Mature S corporation ESOPs often have these characteristics. In this case, a growth strategy to develop new products may be very appropriate, as opportunities for growth are limited within the company's existing business.

Alternatively, the plan might show growth in EBITDA but also dependence on one product or one or two customers to generate profit. While this situation appears healthy, unless the company has contractual exclusivity or unique intellectual property that protects it, this product or customer focus can be risky. This type of plan suggests a business strategy based on product, market, or customer diversification (i.e., a horizontal strategy). Another plan might reflect a very competitive business with no pricing power and with gross profit margin pressure. This type of plan suggests that a consolidation strategy or a cost reduction strategy based on acquiring sources of supply may be appropriate (i.e., a vertical strategy).

The preceding financial plans suggest a need for investment via a build or buy strategy. Depending on the risk appetite and timing considerations, the board may choose an acquisition strategy. This type of strategy may have a big impact on the business in a short period of time. Acquisition strategies can be horizontal to increase revenues or vertical to reduce costs. Some acquisitions, such as the acquisition of a competitor, achieve both.

Typical acquisition strategies can focus on geographic expansion, such as a general construction contractor acquiring other construction contractors in adjacent states. Other strategies involve acquiring related products or services or extending current offerings. An automobile dealer, for example, could acquire multiple car franchises or diversify by acquiring an automotive component supplier. Other strategies can be based on acquiring new products for existing customers. Examples include banks acquiring insurance brokerages and retail brokerages. Similarly, a manufacturer of women's apparel can add a line of men's apparel. Each strategy addresses a particular area of growth, and the proper strategies consider the long-term growth goals the buyer aims to achieve. Identifying the most valuable strategy will be central to efficiently screening and pursuing targets that add the most value.

Acquisition Rubric: Strategy for Target Screening

A useful structure for designing an effective acquisition strategy is to define a rubric of the ideal characteristics of a target, ranked from most to least compelling, and use it to grade opportunities as they present themselves. With the qualities that make a good target top of mind, the buyer will not only be more efficient at screening potential targets recommended by their advisors or identified through their own searches, but will also be able to establish an independent view, constructed by those who operate the business day to day. Targets that meet the threshold score represent opportunities worth investigating; it does not mean these targets will undoubtedly remain as such once further diligence begins, but it provides a numerical standard for the management team to align on and makes it clearer which opportunities are not worth their time.

In all cases, a well-formed strategy evaluates past performance and future growth goals to decide whether the timing is right for an acquisition or whether a build-from-within strategy would be more effective.

The Importance of a Post-Acquisition Integration Strategy

One of the key characteristics of a holistic acquisition strategy is designing a process for integrating the operations, workforce, and culture of the merged entity. Two important cultural differences that often require navigation include compensation and cooperation. For example, a commission-based sales force can think and operate very differently from a salary-plus-bonus sales force, and the cultures of the companies that employ these systems can differ as well. Additionally, if the target company's management team is dissolved in an attempt to merge the oversight of both organizations and save costs, this could lead to instability or even workforce turnover or cultural degradation. Two different systems may not coexist easily; therefore, an integration process may be required to bridge the differences. A dysfunctional culture can create a risk to the acquired revenues, and thus cash flow, if the issues driving the dysfunction are not resolved. Devising a process that considers the impact of an acquisition on all parties involved from a non-financial perspective is crucial to capture and create value post-transaction.

"Cleaning the House": What Makes an Attractive Buyer

Throughout this chapter, we analyze several aspects of acquisition readiness and key areas of understanding from the perspective of the buyer. While it is important throughout the process to consider the seller's psychology, this section steps into the target's shoes to better understand how to position itself as a buyer. While the purchase price is always a prevailing consideration, the buyer's profile is another crucial component. It is not uncommon for business owners, especially families who have owned businesses for generations, to have an emotional investment in the business's continued success. For companies that choose to set up their own ESOPs, common themes owners often seek to preserve are legacy, culture, and a workforce rooted in the company's success. These themes may also be apparent for companies looking to sell to an ESOP-owned company. Often, owners in such situations want to provide an ongoing benefit to reward employees who have played a role in the company's success, or even maintain a level of management control so their life's work is not stripped away post-transaction. Sellers, boards, trustees, lenders, and advisors will evaluate not only the buyer's price but also its ability to close, integrate, and support the acquired business after the transaction, and there are ways a company can "clean its house" to stand out from competitors.

Cleaning the house begins with financial readiness. A buyer that has achieved reliable financial reporting across business units can be viewed as more attractive because it demonstrates that it understands its own business and can identify positive and negative drivers of growth. This may provide a potential seller with confidence that it will not be absorbed into a disorganized or opaque operating environment. Instead, the seller can see that the buyer has a clear process for measuring performance, allocating resources, and supporting growth. Common best practices for internal financial reporting include, but are not limited to:

- Timely monthly reporting and close procedures
- Consistent reporting definitions across business units
- Business-unit-level profitability analysis
- Budget-to-actual and forecast-to-actual comparisons
- Clear tracking of EBITDA, cash flow, working capital, and capital expenditures
- Defined accountability for financial results
- Strong internal controls and review procedures
- Board-ready reporting packages
- Reporting that connects financial results to operating drivers

Furthermore, operational readiness is equally important. Technology is a driver for growth in companies across nearly all industries, and system connectivity can be a key differentiator when cleaning the house. A buyer does not necessarily need every business unit to operate on the same technology platform, but it should understand how its systems communicate with one another and where inefficiencies exist. Finance, accounting, operations, sales, human resources, and customer management systems should provide the management team with a reliable view of the business. Improving systems symbiosis across the business can create value even before an acquisition occurs. Better systems allow management to make faster decisions, identify underperformance earlier, track profitability more accurately, and allocate resources more effectively. They also create a stronger platform for integration. A target company is more likely to view the buyer as a good home if the buyer can demonstrate that its systems will support the business rather than disrupt it.

Organizational structure should also be evaluated before the company enters an acquisition process. A buyer with unclear reporting lines, inconsistent job responsibilities, or overlapping decision-makers may struggle to manage diligence and integration. A more homogeneous organizational structure does not mean every business unit must be identical, but it does mean the company should have a consistent framework for accountability. Organizational structure readiness extends beyond the dynamics of the management team and employees within a company, and it also covers the communication and dynamics between subsidiaries. Splintered ownership structures can be just as much of a deterrent to a seller as they could be to a buyer. Legal, tax, capital markets, and ESOP advisors may be needed to help identify and address governance, financing, benefits, and structural considerations before proceeding with identifying targets, which is discussed later in this chapter.

Communicating Your Strengths as a Buyer

Once the company has improved its own operating foundation, it must be able to communicate why that foundation makes it the right home for a target. Acquisitions are just as much about the target company selling itself as a value-add to the buyer as they are about the buyer selling itself to the target. A buyer's strongest message is often not simply that it wants to acquire the business, but that the buyer has already built the internal systems, processes, and culture needed to help the merged entity succeed after closing. This is where organic improvements become part of the buyer's external story. Advisors should work closely with the buyer to craft a story that highlights how it stands out from other bidders, apart from being able to finance the deal at a particular price, with many of the preparation items listed above being great starting points for those discussions.

Aside from those, a key part of the discussion should focus on the benefits of employee ownership. When the seller is a founder, family-owned company, or an ESOP-owned company, they may care deeply about the company's legacy and the future of its employees. They may want to know that the buyer will not simply impose change for the sake of change, but will bring resources, structure, and stability that help the company grow. They may also be more confident in dealing with the buyer when they know the benefits it provides to its employees, how it treats its employees, and how it adheres to best practices in managing its ESOP. Where the target is not familiar with employee ownership, delivering the message on the benefits of an ESOP and educating the target on the impact it has had on the buyer's employees can be a key differentiator from other bidders. Winning an auction for an acquisition depends heavily on winning the seller's interest from multiple angles, and playing to your strengths and identifying the areas that make your company successful may be effective ways to resonate with the target.

In a competitive process, that distinction can matter. A seller may choose a buyer that offers greater certainty, a stronger cultural fit, and a clearer plan for the future, even if another bid is slightly higher. A buyer that has cleaned its own house and can communicate that preparation effectively is better positioned to earn trust, win the process, and create value after the transaction closes. In this stage and throughout the process, identifying advisors who can effectively communicate that narrative is paramount to achieving success. The next section explains what that means.

Identifying the Right Supporting Cast for Acquisitions

Like any other business activity, acquiring a company requires internal and external resources. A successful acquisition process must include a strategy to describe how the company intends to grow EBITDA (buy or build), identify targets that would meet the objective, price the target, complete due diligence on the target, finance the acquisition, and integrate the acquisition. In addition, there must be a risk management process that assesses the entire transaction.

In general, the acquisition strategy is determined by the CEO, approved by the board, and implemented by the CFO. In some large companies, the entire business development department is devoted to acquisitions. The internal team is most often assisted by the company's lawyers, accountants, and investment bankers.

Before a final offer is made, the company's accountants complete a detailed financial due diligence exercise. The accountants validate the level and quality of the EBITDA that will be bought. They also review the actual and contingent liabilities. If the reported EBITDA is different from the validated EBITDA or the liabilities are understated, the acquirer may pay too high a price. If too high a price is paid, the existing shareholders will be harmed.

Lawyers play a key role in due diligence as well. They review a company's standing, its claims to its assets, its liabilities, its regulatory status, and its litigation and litigation risk. The lawyers then draft a purchase agreement, taking into account this analysis and protecting the acquirer from potential risks identified in both legal and financial due diligence.

The company's investment banker can also play a critical role. In some cases, the banker is hired to find targets for the acquirer. The banker conducts a search according to the criteria specified in the company's acquisition plan. A banker can be effective only if the plan is well-articulated. Broad searches without well-defined criteria are costly and may not be productive.

Additionally, an investment banker is usually hired to help price the acquisition, analyze the impact of the acquisition on value creation, and, in some cases, assist the company with raising capital to finance the acquisition. The same or a different investment bank may also issue a fairness opinion to the board on the purchase price. The board takes this into consideration when determining the price to pay and takes comfort in the fact that it is not overpaying.

Choosing the right team is crucial to achieving success in an acquisition strategy. A group of personnel from the management, finance, accounting, and other teams leads the company's efforts in each phase of the transaction, and they must have the capacity to do so while also fulfilling their day-to-day duties with the company. Investment bankers and lawyers selected should have experience in advising companies in the buyer's region and industry, thus knowing how to navigate the process efficiently while achieving fair values for the purchase prices of targets. Inexperience can create a liability for all parties involved, and the transaction is more susceptible to surprises that could derail the transaction process. This collective, known as the transaction group, must be carefully selected to manage the many moving parts that exist when completing an acquisition.

What's Your Capacity? Debt and Leadership

Like all other capital investments, acquisitions can be financed with internal funds (excess cash), debt capital (senior institutional debt, mezzanine institutional debt, or seller debt), equity capital (preferred stock or common stock), or some combination of these. The type of financing is a function of the debt capacity of both the buyer and the target company. Additionally, it is not uncommon that the type of financing elected is also based on the availability of the capital, whether that is based on industry, company size, or other factors, as well as the costs associated with raising such capital, as the costs (interest rates) associated with financing usually increase the lower you go in seniority.

In general, most acquisitions should be able to be financed by some form of debt without requiring the acquirer to raise equity capital. This should be truer of mature 100% ESOP-owned S corporations, which should have a reasonable amount of excess cash sitting on their balance sheets.

Debt capacity describes a company's borrowing capacity. Debt capacity is measured as a multiple of the borrowing company's EBITDA. Debt capacity varies with the size of a company's EBITDA, the volatility of a company's EBITDA, and the industry in which a company operates. Total debt capacity is the sum of both senior debt capacity and junior debt capacity. Senior debt capacity reflects the amount of senior debt that a company can borrow, given its EBITDA, and junior debt capacity reflects the multiple of EBITDA on top of the senior debt that a junior lender will add. In normal credit markets, it is not unusual to see total debt capacity up to 4.5x EBITDA, with 2.5x to 3.0x allocated to senior debt and the balance allocated to junior debt. In strong liquid markets, with lower-than-normal interest rates, these numbers can go higher.

Available debt capacity is the difference between a company's existing debt load and its total debt capacity. A portion of a company's available debt capacity should be held in reserve, "just in case." To be clear, a company should never use 100% of its debt capacity by borrowing. It should always have some "dry powder" for a rainy day.

Acquisitions can enhance debt capacity because the buyer can borrow using both its available debt capacity and the target's available debt capacity. In addition, there is a possibility that debt capacity expansion can occur if the resulting combined EBITDA from the acquisition brings the company into an EBITDA range where, given the new size and scale, lenders are willing to take more risk. Understanding this concept is a key factor in building an effective strategy that enables companies to acquire larger targets than they normally would be able to.

In addition to debt capacity, another important capacity to consider is that of the leadership team involved in the process. In tandem with navigating the twists and turns of the M&A process, the management team must not only be able to maintain the operations of the business but also continue to grow it. Growth will only increase the confidence of lenders in terms of providing larger amounts of acquisition financing with more favorable terms. This, in turn, enables the company to submit larger bids or provide the target with confidence that the bid is supportable, which could be the difference between making it to the final discussions and winning the acquisition. Allocating the right personnel internally and devising a strategy in which they can perform their duties to the company and support each stage of the transaction process is paramount to an effective acquisition process.

The M&A Process from Start to Finish

Once the management team has prepared the company internally and developed an acquisition strategy, the next step is translating that strategy into a disciplined acquisition process. As stated above, acquisitions can be a resource-intensive process, consuming time and focus away from key leaders that could be used to operate and improve the business organically. The management team must be knowledgeable about the process so it can allocate its executives' time efficiently while maximizing the transaction's outcome. Surprises will only delay closing and add complexity.

Once a target is identified and matches the criteria outlined in the acquisition strategy, the next step is preliminary evaluation. At this stage, the management team and company advisors (collectively, the "buyer") will work together to determine whether the acquisition is strategically logical and financially feasible before investing significant time and resources. After gaining access to the target's information through both parties (buyer and target) signing non-disclosure agreements, the buyer will evaluate the key investment considerations of the target. This includes, but is not limited to, revenues, EBITDA, marginal growth rates, customer concentration, working capital needs, synergies realized through a merger, leadership team, and cultural fit. The buyer should also consider whether the target would be integrated into the existing business, operated as a separate division, or used as a platform for additional growth. This early analysis does not replace due diligence, but it helps determine whether the opportunity is worth pursuing further.

If the buyer decides to proceed, the next step is often a non-binding indication of interest (IOI). The IOI sets out a broad valuation range for the target and cements the buyer's interest in pursuing the transaction. Proper due diligence is required to develop a valuation range that is neither so low in comparison to other bids that the buyer is taken out of the running, nor so high that it becomes harder for the buyer to walk back its range when producing its next bid. Upon moving to the next round, a more in-depth due diligence phase begins, with management presentations and site visits, as well as access to the target's information through a virtual data room. In developing the next bid, there are key areas of non-financial due diligence that must be considered, including legal challenges, workforce/management team integration, and estimates on the competition/financial positioning of other buyers participating to decide how much to price the bid and whether to submit it at all. Discussions with financing sources usually begin during this phase. If the buyer decides to move forward, it will submit a letter of intent (LOI), which outlines how much they intend to pay for the target, how they will pay for it, and other go-forward considerations that the buyer would want to make the target aware of.

If the buyer's bid is the most attractive of the pool, then the target will sign the LOI and move forward into an exclusivity phase in which further diligence is collected, often more intensive than the preceding diligence phases. The buyer needs to be highly confident that the information being presented is aligned with its expectations from earlier in the process. During this time, the terms of the definitive agreements, most notably the purchase agreement, are heavily negotiated by the legal counsel of both parties to ensure the transaction is fair and reasonable. Once diligence is completed, legal documents are finalized, financing sources are secured, and any necessary approvals are obtained, the transaction can be completed with the proper transfers taking place. Throughout this entire process, the selected subset of the company designated as the transaction support will be heavily engaged at times and will be interfacing regularly with the advisor group to ensure that the transaction stays on track. Efficient time allocation is required to balance the priorities of reaching transaction milestones while operating the business simultaneously.

The most common hurdles often arrive in the second half of the process, and this is a key point to be aware of before it begins. Even a good acquisition can become risky if the execution is not treated carefully. Debt capacity, working capital needs, transaction expenses, integration costs, and the timing of synergy realization all affect whether the acquisition can be financed prudently. The buyer should test the transaction under downside cases, not only under the base case. In addition, the buyer should identify and strategize the process steps that take longer and those that take more effort to move forward. For example, getting ahead of financing processes, regulatory requirements, and approval requirements early could mean the difference between a successful and an unsuccessful transaction. A buyer does not need to resolve every point before a target is screened, but timing can easily derail a close, so it benefits the buyer to try to get ahead of these items before they begin to increase the certainty of completing the transaction.

Considerations for ESOP Companies and ESOP-to-ESOP Mergers

ESOP companies must consider all the ordinary issues involved in acquisitions, on top of how the transaction affects the ESOP, the participants, the trustee, the board of directors, and the company's repurchase obligation going forward. To complete the transaction, ESOP companies must seek proper approvals from the trustee and board, as well as be able to prove that the acquisition will not harm the accrued benefits of current participants in the plan, as that would create a lawsuit liability for the parties involved. If the acquired employees are brought into the buyer's ESOP, the value and future obligations will be spread across a larger group of participants. If they are not included, the benefit and the repurchase obligation may be concentrated among the buyer's existing participants. Additionally, if the acquisition increases the value of the buyer's stock, that increase may also increase future repurchase obligations.

Benefit alignment also matters; many ESOP companies have retirement and compensation practices that are more generous than those of non-ESOP companies. If the buyer intends to bring the target's employees into the same benefit structure, the cost of doing so should be analyzed as part of diligence and valuation.

ESOP-to-ESOP mergers add another level of complexity because the transaction involves not only two companies but also two employee ownership structures and potentially two fiduciary processes. The early stages, however, are very similar to an acquisition process for a non-ESOP target company. The buyer trustee and target trustee are generally not involved in these initial negotiations, and do not need to be notified until much later in the transaction process. Their role, if required, is to evaluate the transaction presented to them, not to negotiate the business deal. This distinction matters because the board, officers, trustees, and shareholders each have different roles under corporate law and ERISA.

In a stock-for-stock ESOP acquisition, the buyer may exchange newly issued buyer shares for the target ESOP's shares of target stock. The target then becomes a wholly owned subsidiary of the buyer, and the target ESOP holds buyer stock until the target ESOP is merged into the buyer ESOP. This structure makes valuation and relative fairness a key point of diligence in the transaction. The buyer must conduct normal diligence to determine the value of the target and the appropriate exchange ratio for the respective shares. The target, in turn, must conduct reverse diligence to determine the value of the shares it will receive from the buyer. If the target's shares are dilutive to the value of the buyer, and by proxy the buyer's ESOP and the shares of participants in the buyer's plan, then approval for the transaction becomes much more difficult, even if there is synergistic value to be realized. In light of this, the target ESOP trustee may request buyer financial information and engage a financial advisor to provide a fairness opinion. The buyer trustee's role may be more limited because the buyer ESOP may not be directly acquiring anything, although the buyer should communicate clearly with the buyer trustee regarding any approval, monitoring, or involvement requirements.

Several plan-level and closing issues should be addressed early. The parties must determine the required board approvals, whether state law requires shareholder action, whether pass-through voting applies, and how the ESOP plans will be merged. Using stock as consideration does not automatically require a pass-through vote, and pass-through voting depends on the corporate action, state law, and the shares allocated to participant accounts. The parties must also address the outstanding ESOP loans, unallocated shares, collateral, debt assumption or repayment, repurchase obligations, synthetic equity agreements, post-closing plan administration, and more. Communicating the merger to employees is also critical to maintain alignment in the workforce because the ESOP will be affected, especially if the price of participants' shares falls due to the transaction. After closing, the companies must integrate operations, management teams, systems, benefits, ESOP administration, and culture. The objective is not simply to transfer shares from one ESOP to another, but to create a stronger combined company that can sustain and grow value while preserving the economic and cultural benefits of employee ownership.

Conclusion

Acquisitions *may* be an important component of growing value for an ESOP, but only if each component is properly analyzed and the strategy for pursuing the transaction is built on a strong foundation. If the process fails, it can be a huge blow to the company's momentum and an immense waste of time and money for its key leaders, so a diligent process throughout is paramount. A strong foundation grows from understanding the company's value and the valuation of targets, assessing whether the company is ready for acquisitions, evaluating its leadership and capital capacity, and understanding the M&A process to avoid surprises. Increasing the certainty of a transaction close includes reducing areas that can cause disruptions, and being knowledgeable in all three of these areas beforehand makes achieving that possible while investing in quality assets that create long-term value. That is the true benefit of a disciplined acquisition strategy.

CHAPTER 2

Managing Risk

Lynn DuBois

THE DECISION to acquire another company is a "bet-the-company" decision for the board of the acquiring company. Understanding the risks and rewards of the bet is crucial for the acquiring company and involves a thorough understanding of the board's fiduciary duties to its shareholders, a complete and detailed due diligence process, and, for an ESOP shareholder, an assessment of any involvement that may be required of the ESOP trustee.

Due Diligence and the Purchase Agreement

The diligence process is designed to investigate and evaluate a business opportunity. It is a time-consuming process that requires collaboration among the target company, the acquiring company, and their respective legal advisors. Through the diligence process, the acquiring company will perform a thorough investigation of the target to gain a thorough understanding of the target's business and identify the target's real or potential liabilities to recognize and minimize the acquiring company's risk and to avoid overpaying for the target. A successful acquisition depends upon a thorough and thoughtful diligence process, which comprises business, financial, and legal due diligence designed to examine all material aspects of the target company's business.

Business Diligence and Reputation Risk

Boards should have clear acquisition strategies (as discussed above) and should investigate and understand every aspect of the target company's business. A board should have an understanding of why the shareholders are selling, the strategic fit, the synergies that will be obtained by combining the companies, and how the target business will be integrated into the acquiring company's business. Boards should fully evaluate and document all execution risks, including the risk of the acquirer's failure to obtain financing.

Boards also should understand any reputational risk associated with the acquisition. Most companies are well aware that a company's business reputation is a very valuable intangible asset that must be protected. Risks to a company's reputation can come from internal or external sources. Poor or unethical performance by the board or an employee, failure to meet financial targets, regulatory compliance failures, or a product recall can tarnish a company's good business reputation.

A company with a good business reputation will have in place a risk-management team, with members from every level of the organization, a risk-management assessment program appropriate for its business and industry, and a response plan. Both internal risks and external risks will be monitored and responded to. The chief financial officer will monitor financial risks. The director of human resources will monitor hiring decisions and employment policies. The chief operating officer will monitor vendor and supply chains. The chief executive officer and other members of the board will monitor business strategies, including the company's acquisition strategy. Many companies employ a chief risk officer (CRO), who will work with and oversee the other members of the risk management team to help identify risks and plan appropriate risk responses.

As part of the board's acquisition strategy and the diligence process, the acquiring company will evaluate reputation risks that could arise from the acquisition, either from the target business itself or as a result of the combination of the two businesses. As part of its acquisition strategy, the board must assess the target company's culture, value, and overall fit with the acquirer. The target's risk management program (or lack thereof) should be reviewed. As part of the diligence process, the board will need to analyze the target company's responses to the financial, legal, and other diligence and consider the impact of any discovered reputation risks.

Financial Diligence

Financial due diligence is conducted to enable the acquiring company to determine the accuracy of the financial information received during the diligence process. Financial due diligence is important for examining accounting information that affects current and future earnings ("quality of earnings") and for identifying future growth opportunities. In smaller transactions, the financial diligence is often conducted by the acquiring company's own financial team. For very large transactions, the acquirer will engage an accounting or valuation firm to examine the target's accounting practices, review the target's business plan, analyze the target's cash flow, and assess industry competition. The financial diligence team will analyze historical financial statements and other financial information, tax returns, future projections, and financial performance metrics such as gross margin, debt/equity ratio, and working capital requirements. The financial diligence will identify inconsistent accounting practices and test the estimates and judgments used by the target company in its future projections.

Legal Diligence

Legal due diligence differs from other types of diligence, such as financial or tax, in that its focus is limited to legal matters and does not aim to analyze business issues. Instead, the legal due diligence process raises certain legal issues and provides a risk assessment to the acquiring company for use in its business decisions. For example, the acquirer's legal counsel will likely review the target company's material contracts to analyze termination and indemnification provisions as well as to determine whether any consents or notices are required as a result of the transaction. However, the acquiring company will also review the same contracts from a business perspective with an emphasis on revenue, cost, profitability, etc.

The diligence request. The acquiring company will begin the legal diligence by delivering to the target company (or its counsel) a legal diligence request list (also referred to as a diligence checklist). The diligence request will be divided into several categories (described in more detail below) and will contain specific requests for documents or information relating to each topic. Some diligence requests can be incredibly long and detailed, while others may be brief or concentrate mostly on a few topics. The size and detail of the diligence request depends on the circumstances of and budget for the transaction, such as the acquiring company's knowledge of the target company, the industry involved, the size of the transaction both in dollar amounts and the percentage of ownership being purchased, and the timeline of the transaction (a more extensive diligence request and related diligence review will require a longer timeline for the transaction close).

While an acquirer wants to obtain as much information as possible about the target company to assist in determining the appropriate purchase price and provide sufficient comfort in completing the transaction, the practical limitations of time and money often serve as a prohibition on unlimited requests.

Virtual data room. Once the diligence request has been delivered and the target company begins assembling its responses to the requests, a virtual data room (VDR) will be created. A VDR is a cloud-based data collection point that allows the target (or its counsel) to upload materials to one location that the acquiring company and its advisors can access to review the documents. A VDR usually will be the most efficient method of delivering documents to multiple parties (rather than copying and faxing or mailing documents). An additional advantage of a VDR is that the target company may assign different settings to each document or folder to enable only certain parties access to particular items. For example, a target may want to control who has access to its financial statements, material contracts, or personnel files.

Diligence meeting. As part of the legal diligence process, the acquiring company often sends its legal counsel to visit the target company's headquarters and/or its main operations for on-site diligence review.

Diligence review is sometimes conducted on-site when the target's files and materials are extensive and/or not well organized for scanning and uploading to a VDR. Diligence review is often conducted on-site in conjunction with data collection in a VDR to both enhance and speed up the diligence review. The diligence reviewer(s) can meet with the target company's key personnel, who can immediately answer questions and provide thorough descriptions and explanations of items that would be more difficult to resolve and take more time if done in a series of email exchanges and conference calls.

Supplemental diligence requests. After the target company has provided responses to the diligence request and the acquiring company has begun its review of the materials, the acquirer will often prepare and submit supplemental diligence requests. The supplemental diligence requests usually will include outstanding requests and incomplete responses from the initial diligence request as well as new requests that arise as a result of newly discovered information or from issues raised during the diligence meeting or diligence review.

The diligence process can be a long, drawn-out process and sometimes seem never-ending, especially for target employees who must respond to many requests, assemble hundreds of documents, and provide a considerable amount of information. The target company will often complain, sometimes not without reason, that the requests for information and documents are overly burdensome and that responding to all of the requests takes enormous amounts of time. The number of requests and the level of detail requested often will be a subject of negotiation between the acquiring company and the target company, but with consultation between the acquiring company and its legal counsel, the requisite diligence can be gathered, allowing the acquirer to gain a thorough understanding of the target and its legal issues without unnecessarily antagonizing the target.

Legal Due Diligence Topics

The following is a summary of the major legal due diligence topics and a description of some of the more common issues associated with them.

The following list is by no means exhaustive but rather covers topics that generally will be included in the diligence request for any transaction.

Corporate documents; organizational matters. The acquiring company will review the target company's corporate charter (articles or certificate of incorporation) and bylaws, including any amendments, as well as board of directors and shareholder meeting minutes and written consents. The acquirer will confirm that the target company is registered to conduct business and is in good standing in each jurisdiction where the target conducts business.

Company records are not always as well-kept as they should be, so it is important to confirm that the target company has provided all material actions by the board or shareholders, especially in the most recent three years, and that any amendments to the corporate charter have actually been filed with the secretary of state where the target company is incorporated.

Shareholder information and documents. The acquiring company will review the target company's stock ledger to identify the shareholders and how many shares of each class of stock each shareholder owns; analyze any options, warrants, or other equity (synthetic or otherwise) that the target has granted or issued; and confirm whether there are any buy-sell or shareholder agreements, voting trusts, or other limits on the voting or transfer of the target company's stock.

Many privately held companies have shareholder agreements that restrict the transfer of company stock or provide for rights of first refusal in the event of the sale of stock, but companies sometimes allow shareholders to transfer company stock without following the correct procedures. The acquiring company should properly review past stock transfers to ensure that no shareholder claim arises from past sales or transfers.

Contracts (non-intellectual property). Contracts are usually broken out into separate groups—customer contracts, supplier/vendor contracts, leases, business contracts (which typically include service agreements and agency or distribution agreements), and other contracts. Depending on the nature of the target company's business, some of those groupings can include hundreds or even thousands of agreements, especially if the contracts are ongoing and include many exhibits and amendments.

Often, the target company will push back on the request if the response requires the target company to scan or copy thousands of pages of contracts, much of which could be considered boilerplate. As a compromise, the parties often will agree on a reasonable contract threshold limit, and the target will provide copies of the agreements in amounts above that threshold amount (commonly referred to as "material contracts"). The threshold is usually an annual dollar amount per contract and/or a total per-contract dollar amount.

The target company will make representations and warranties regarding all of the contracts (including both the material contracts that were provided to the acquiring company for review as well as the immaterial contracts that were not reviewed). The contracts will be reviewed for, among other things, any consents or notices required as a result of the transaction, whether the contracts can be terminated, what the cost would be to terminate, and what the target's rights and liabilities are in connection with the agreements (indemnification provisions, noncompetition provisions, etc.).

Many leases and sophisticated contracts require the consent of the other party in the event of a change in control of a party. Obtaining such consents often requires a long lead time, so it is best to start a contract diligence review as soon as possible. Doing so will avoid having to delay the closing at the last minute when the parties learn that the only person who can sign off on the consent is unavailable during the closing period.

Credit and financings. The acquiring company will review all of the credit arrangements of the target company that will remain in place after the closing (and usually review any financings that are being paid off at closing) to gain a clear understanding of the target company's obligations as well as any restrictions the loans place on the business, such as incurring additional debt or paying bonuses. A search for any financing statements filed against the target should be performed to analyze what liens, including tax liens, have been placed on the target's property.

Obtaining consents from major banks can take a very long time, depending on the company's relationships at the bank. It is very important to review bank consent requirements early in the diligence process because even a 25% change in the voting power of a borrower generally will require lender consent.

Litigation. It is imperative for the acquiring company to have a complete understanding of all litigation involving the target company (as plaintiff or defendant), as well as any complaints or threats that create any potential for future litigation. Copies of any complaints or proceedings should be reviewed, and conversations with the target company's in-house and outside counsel should be arranged, especially for any material litigation or potential litigation. It is also important to request copies of any settlements or judgments involving the target company within the last three to five years.

Depending on the nature of the target company's business, a thorough review of its employment practices should be considered, especially with regard to any potential exposure to wage and hour class-action claims from current or former employees.

Real property. A review of the target company's real property, whether owned or leased (including the length and other terms of any lease), is especially important if the target's business is dependent on that property and its location. While a financial services company that leases office space in a downtown city location will not require a very detailed real property diligence review, a manufacturing company that has a special land use variance for its premises to conduct its operations will require a thorough review. A search for any liens, including tax liens, should be performed.

As with any real property, especially if the premises have been in use for a long period of time, attention must be paid to any encroachments, easements, or defects of title. There are also environmental issues that may need to be addressed, even if the target company leases and does not own the premises.

Environmental matters. The acquiring company should review the target company's environmental records, including any hazardous materials used, stored, or disposed of on the target company's real property or in the course of the target's business. Similar to the real property review, the scope of the diligence is dependent on the nature of the target's business. Any Phase I reports that have been performed on target property should be reviewed.

Depending on the nature of the target company's business and what the initial diligence review reveals, an environmental expert may need to be retained to obtain a complete understanding of the risks associated with the target company's environmental issues.

Intellectual property. The acquiring company will need to review any registered intellectual property of the target company (copyrights, trademarks, and patents) as well as copies of any licensing agreements. If the target company has developed any proprietary software or code, the acquiring company will need to review any independent contractor agreements for work that was performed by a non-employee and any assignment of invention agreements for any work that was performed by employees. Information relating to domain names, websites, and social media also will need to be obtained and reviewed.

Smaller companies (and some large companies) will hire outside contractors (and sometimes use employees outside of their normal duties with the company) to help create or design company intellectual property, such as software programs, logos and brand names, and social media sites. It is important to ensure that the target company completely owns the resulting intellectual property and that the contractor cannot make a valid claim of ownership.

Insurance. The acquiring company should review the target company's insurance policies even if the acquirer plans to terminate the policies following the closing.

Depending on the nature of the target company's business, the acquiring company should pay special attention to whether the target's insurance coverage is claims-made or occurrence-based to determine what potential exposure exists if the policies are cancelled.

Tax matters. The diligence request will include copies of the target company's federal and state tax returns as well as information regarding past or current audits or examinations.

Labor and personnel matters. The acquiring company should request an employee census and review the target company's employee handbook, any employment letters or employment agreements, and any agreements with independent contractors or agents of the target company. As mentioned previously, it is important for the acquiring company to have an understanding of the target's employment practices in relation to breaks, overtime, exempt/nonexempt classifications, and employee/independent contractor classifications. The diligence request will also include requests for descriptions of target company policies with regard to termination and severance, incentives and bonuses, and fringe benefits. Any collective bargaining agreements will need to be reviewed.

Any agreements between the target company and its employees, contractors, or agents (including any severance or release agreements) need to be analyzed for provisions that include nonsolicitation and noncompetition restrictions to determine whether and how such agreements will affect the acquiring company following the transaction.

Employee benefit plans. The diligence request should request all employee benefit plans (qualified, nonqualified, health and welfare plans, etc.) as well as information regarding any Department of Labor, Internal Revenue Service, or other governmental agency investigations or requests for information.

Financial statements. The acquiring company should request at least the prior three years of financial statements, including footnotes, and copies of monthly and quarterly financials for the current year.

Other matters. Other topics that may require review and further investigation include, but are not limited to, permits and licenses of the target company, antitrust matters, detailed asset listings, foreign law matters (such as FCPA, taxes, and importing/exporting), government contracting, and government regulation (for businesses regulated by federal agencies such as the SEC, the FDA, and the FAA).

The Purchase Agreement

There are multiple transaction structures that can be used for acquisitions, as discussed below, but regardless of the transaction structure used, there will be a definitive purchase agreement. Common to all purchase agreements are several sections that directly relate to managing risk by allocating whether the acquiring company or the target company bears the risk and to what extent. Entire chapters can be written about purchase agreements, but this section will provide a high-level summary of three major portions of the purchase agreement that directly relate to managing risk.

Target Representations and Warranties

The purchase agreement will include representations and warranties to the acquiring company by the selling shareholders regarding their shares and the condition of the target company itself (the "reps and warranties" for short). Many of the reps and warranties are considered to be standard in almost all purchase agreements, while others depend on the industry and the actual facts and circumstances of the target company. The reps and warranties are heavily negotiated because they are the primary means of allocating risk between the acquirer and the target's selling shareholders. The reps and warranties require the target company and its shareholders to make certain factual representations about the target.

The reps and warranties are qualified by the disclosure schedules, which set forth any exceptions to the reps and warranties. The reps and warranties and the disclosure schedules work hand in hand to create a record of the selling shareholders' statements of facts about the target company, which, if untrue, create liability after closing for the target shareholders under the indemnification provisions described below. For example, a common representation is "except as set forth on the Disclosure Schedules, the target company is not a party to any

Litigation nor, to the target's knowledge, are there any facts or circumstances that could reasonably be expected to result in Litigation." If there are any facts that would make this representation untrue, those facts should be listed on the disclosure schedule so that the acquiring company is made aware of them.

If it turns out that the target company is a party to any litigation that is not disclosed on the disclosure schedules but should have been disclosed, the acquiring company can pursue the selling shareholders for damages pursuant to the indemnification provisions. The reps and warranties and disclosure schedules should be drafted as early as possible in the negotiation process of the purchase agreement because they can affect the business terms of the deal.

Material Indemnification Provisions

All purchase agreements include provisions that provide for indemnification of the acquiring company in the event the target company or its selling shareholders breach the reps and warranties. There are many different ways to structure indemnification provisions, but the following three provisions will be in every form of purchase agreement and are the most visible methods of risk allocation. When the acquiring company seeks indemnification from the target company's selling shareholders for a breach of the reps and warranties (i.e., when it makes a claim), certain limitations are negotiated. Just because the acquiring company makes a claim, however, does not mean that the acquiring company will automatically be able to collect the claimed amount from the selling shareholders; the selling shareholders may deny any liability or dispute the amount. It is not unusual for claims to end up in litigation.

- *Basket.* The basket sets the minimum threshold for claims before the selling shareholders have to pay the acquiring company for breaches. Once the aggregate amount of claims crosses over the threshold (i.e., the basket), the acquirer can use certain methods of recovering its damages (set-off from other monies owed to the selling shareholders, escrow claims, litigation, etc.). The basket is a negotiated amount that provides that the selling shareholders will not be required to pay for an immaterial amount of claims (there are usually exceptions for fraud and some levels of negligence or intentional breaches) while providing comfort to the acquiring company that it will be indemnified for material amounts.

- *Cap.* The cap is usually negotiated in tandem with the basket (and to a certain extent with the survival period described below) and provides the maximum amount of claims for which the selling shareholders will be liable. The cap ranges anywhere from 10% of the purchase price to 100% and often contains exceptions for certain specified items that are of particular concern to the acquiring company. For example, if environmental or tax issues were discovered during the diligence process that were unquantifiable at closing, the acquiring company might insist on a complete indemnification for those items—with no cap. As with the basket, there are usually exceptions to the cap amount for fraud and some levels of negligence or intentional breaches.
- *Survival period.* The survival period is the period of time following the closing of the transaction during which the acquiring company can seek indemnification from the selling shareholders for claims. Usually, a survival period is set (12, 18, or 24 months) for the majority of claims, with a longer time period set (generally for the period of the applicable statute of limitations) for claims involving certain reps and warranties such as tax, environmental, and employee benefits. Other reps and warranties, such as ownership of the shares, are deemed to be so fundamental to the transaction that the period for claims related to these reps and warranties never expires.

Fiduciary Issues for the Board of Directors

A company's board of directors is a fiduciary for the benefit of the company's shareholders, and a board should approve an acquisition only if the board determines that the acquisition is in the best interests of the shareholders. In most cases, the board will be protected by the business judgment rule, which is the presumption that the board acted in an informed manner ("duty of care"), in the best interests of the company and its shareholders ("duty of loyalty"), and in good faith.

The underlying principle of the business judgment rule is that a court will not substitute its judgment for that of the board if the board's decision can be attributed to any rational purpose. To prevent boards from being overly concerned about after-the-fact second-guessing claims by shareholders who have the benefit of hindsight, courts are very deferential to a board's decisions in applying the business judgment rule. A court will not find a board liable solely for unfavorable results. To take advantage of the protection provided by the business judgment rule, directors need to comply with their fiduciary duties and maintain a record of their decision-making process. Courts have held that in addition to the duties of care and loyalty, a board must act in good faith in taking any action.

The duty of care requires a member of the board to make business decisions based on all available and material information and to act in a deliberate and informed manner. The test applied by courts also includes a requirement that the board act as prudent persons would act in similar circumstances. The board should consider all available information and should avoid hasty decision-making (or even the appearance of hasty decision-making). The board may rely on the advice of independent experts, but the directors must make a reasonable inquiry into the facts on which such experts base their advice and must consider whether any person providing information might be biased based on a fee arrangement.

The duty of loyalty is essentially a requirement that members of the board must act in the best interests of the company, and by extension its shareholders, and not in their own interest. The board's duty of loyalty includes a prohibition against a director profiting from a transaction at the expense of the company and its shareholders. However, a corporate transaction in which a director has a material financial interest will not be invalid if the transaction is fair to the company and if the material terms of the transaction and the director's interest are disclosed to, and ratified by, the disinterested shareholders or by disinterested directors acting in good faith. This duty of loyalty is an issue that can arise in privately held companies with few shareholders where the board is at least partially composed of directors who are also shareholders. When this overlap occurs, the board and the company need to proceed cautiously when contemplating a transaction that also involves an interested director.

Even in the context of "bet-the-company" acquisitions, courts have held that the protection afforded by the business judgment rule will apply and that heightened scrutiny of director decision-making will not apply to good-faith decisions made by a majority of disinterested directors, regardless of the size or importance of the transaction, or the potential impact on the buyer and its shareholders if the deal fails. Courts will review the board's decision-making process to determine whether the board acted in an informed manner, in the best interests of the company and its shareholders, and in good faith.

A good decision-making process will help ensure that a board's decision to acquire another company will not be second-guessed, absent a "complete and utter failure" to review the merits of the acquisition decision itself.

Issues for Trustees to Consider

When an ESOP company acquires another company, there are certain issues that arise for the trustee as a shareholder. The major consideration for the trustee will be to determine what level of involvement it will have in the transaction and what the effect on the ESOP will be.

Shareholder Approval

The acquisition may not require shareholder approval. Stock purchase transactions do not require shareholder approval by the acquiring company's shareholders. If the ESOP company is purchasing the stock of another company, there is no requirement that the ESOP company obtain shareholder approval (though the target company could make approval by the acquirer's shareholders a closing condition). If the transaction is structured as a merger, however, shareholder approval will be required under relevant state corporate law.

Section 409(e) of the Internal Revenue Code requires voting pass-through by the ESOP to the ESOP participants if the applicable state law requires a shareholder vote. However, many states, including California and Delaware, allow mergers by the consent of a simple majority. This means that in states that permit merger approval by written consent of the majority shareholders, if the ESOP owns less than 50% of the outstanding voting power, the merger will be approved without needing the ESOP's vote, which means the voting pass-through requirement will not be triggered.

Dilution of the ESOP

Even in transactions that do not require shareholder approval, trustees should inquire whether the transaction will result in new shares of company stock being issued, such as would be the case in a stock-for-stock transaction or a merger that provides company stock as all or part of the consideration. If the ESOP owns over 50% of the company before such transactions, the trustee must determine whether any dilution takes the ESOP from a majority ownership position to a minority position.

Effect on ESOP Obligations

If the transaction will add new financing obligations to the ESOP company, the trustee should evaluate the effect of the increased debt on future ESOP contributions and benefit distributions. Section 409(e) permits deferral of ESOP benefit distributions only until the ESOP's stock acquisition loan is repaid but does not provide such deferral for other company financings.

ERISA requires the trustee to act with the care, skill, prudence, and diligence under the circumstances then prevailing that a prudent person acting in a like capacity and familiar with such matters would use in taking action. The trustee should be aware of a proposed acquisition by its company, but depending on the circumstances (transaction size, ESOP ownership percentage, structure of transaction, etc.), the trustee's involvement may range from little more than having knowledge of the transaction to having its counsel review the due diligence of the target company and review and comment on the transaction documents.

No matter what action a trustee determines to take or not to take, a thoughtful and well-documented decision-making process will be the best evidence of the trustee's prudent decision-making and the best response to any audit or investigation by the Department of Labor or a court challenge. The trustee will be judged not on the outcome of the transaction but on the reasonableness and prudence of the decisions made under the circumstances and at the time of the acquisition.

CHAPTER 3

Using ESOPs in Mergers and Acquisitions

William W. Merten

ESOPS set up within a company have long provided an exit strategy for owners of privately held businesses. Increasingly, ESOP companies themselves have been acquiring other companies. This chapter discusses ESOP acquisitions, together with related planning considerations, structures, corporate governance issues, and financing concerns.

General Planning Considerations

Consideration by the Board of Directors

Acquisition opportunities are usually (but not always) brought to the attention of a company's board by one or more members of its management team. In determining whether the company should offer to purchase another entity, the board is legally responsible for acting in the interests of all shareholders. In undertaking this responsibility, board decisions are generally judged by applying the "business judgment rule," which permits a company's board members to apply their reasonable business judgment in deciding whether to pursue offers (with "business judgment" case law being developed and applied on a state-by-state basis).

Consideration by Trustee(s)

An ESOP trustee is charged with acting solely in the interest of plan participants and beneficiaries and for the exclusive purpose of providing retirement benefits. Given this charge, even in a company wholly owned by an ESOP, an ESOP trustee may have slightly different responsibilities than the company's board regarding a company purchase offer. While a board's determination is judged by applying the above-described business judgment rule, the trustee is held to ERISA fiduciary standards.

Transaction Types

Once the decision is made to pursue an acquisition opportunity, the acquisition will generally be structured in one of three ways. As more fully described below, the acquiring company can (1) buy the stock or the assets of the division or company, (2) merge with the division or company, or (3) have the target company or division create a new ESOP, sell itself to the ESOP, and then merge the new ESOP with the acquirer's existing ESOP.

Due Diligence and Key Acquisition Terms

While important, arriving at a price agreeable to both parties to an acquisition is usually not the most difficult part of the transaction. Indeed, the time spent negotiating the purchase price will often pale compared to the time spent by the purchaser in completing thorough due diligence and the time spent by both parties in negotiating escrows, indemnifications, clawbacks, and ongoing executive compensation.

ESOP Trustee Oversight

If an ESOP trustee determines that an acquisition will be sizable (e.g., more than 10% of the acquirer's value), the trustee may request to be involved in the acquisition process. The trustee may want to participate in due diligence and may want to receive an opinion from its independent financial advisor that the acquisition is fair to the ESOP from a financial viewpoint. For larger transactions, the board may want to receive a similar opinion (as to fairness to all shareholders) from its own financial advisor. Although the trustee and the acquirer company will each be concerned with holding down acquisition costs, the trustee must preserve the independence of its financial advisor. It may be appropriate for the acquirer's board to consider having its own financial advisor (i.e., one different from the trustee's advisor).

A company partially or wholly owned by an ESOP may have appointed inside employee(s) as ESOP trustee(s). When a major acquisition is in the offing, inside trustees may have conflicts of interest regarding one or more aspects of the potential acquisition and thus may have trouble properly fulfilling applicable ERISA fiduciary duties. Should such conflicts arise, consideration should be given to the propriety of appointing either independent trustee(s) or having an independent or institutional trustee serve as an independent fiduciary who will direct the inside trustee(s) concerning the acquisition.

Cultural Fit

The acquirer's board will, of course, consider the strategic fit of the target company. It should also consider the cultural fit of the two organizations. Many studies suggest that this cultural fit is the most important contributor to the future success or failure of an acquisition.

Continuation, Termination, or Possible Merger of Existing Target Plans

In almost every M&A transaction, the acquirer must consider the disposition of existing (non-ESOP) retirement plans at the target company. The plans can either be (1) continued with amendments, (2) terminated, or (3) merged into the acquirer's existing plans. If they are continued with amendments, basic principles of plan participation, vesting, and retirement will continue to apply. These principles can give rise to multiple plan issues (e.g., minimum coverage, combined plan limits, or using dividends or distributions to sidestep applicable limits).

If the plans are merged, the acquirer must also review the target plans for possible plan and/or statutory violations. The acquirer does not want existing acquirer plans to become tainted with problems from the target plans.

If a target plan is instead terminated, its participants will become immediately vested and eligible for distributions. This can have the unintended effect of potentially placing considerable sums of money in the hands of financially inexperienced employees, possibly resulting in unexpected defections from the target employee workforce.

Finally, a decision must be made about participation by target employees in the acquirer's ESOP. If the acquirer desires to exclude target employees from its ESOP, the exclusion must comply with applicable coverage and/or separate-line-of-business requirements.[1] If, alternatively, the acquirer is prepared to bring target employees into its ESOP, decisions will have to be made regarding timing for participation and service to be counted for eligibility and vesting (with such decisions significantly affecting the acquirer's repurchase obligation, plan benefit levels, and compliance testing).

Valuation Concerns

A successful acquisition will positively affect the buyer's long-term stock price. In the near term, however, if the acquirer uses cash to wholly or partially finance an acquisition, there may be a significant temporary negative effect on the acquirer's cash flow or its ability to make necessary capital expenditures or handle upcoming repurchase obligations. The buyer might also grant equity rights to certain target company employees, which would dilute the stock value. It is possible that factors such as these could lower the share price of the acquirer's stock, usually on a temporary basis, until the acquisition starts to add positive cash flow to the buyer. Should this occur, the acquirer may decide to amend the plan to provide that the company will make price

1. With regard to compliance testing, first see Section 410(b)(6)(c) of the Internal Revenue Code. As to separate lines of business, first see Treas. Reg. § 1.414(r)5(d) for the safe harbor for separate lines of business acquired through certain mergers and acquisitions.

protection payments for certain ESOP participants whose employment may be terminated before the debt can be repaid. If it does, it will also have to determine (1) the length of the protection (e.g., whether it will last for a set period of years or until the acquisition indebtedness is repaid in its entirety), (2) the members of the protected class (e.g., whether the class will include employees who are terminated due to death, disability, and/or normal retirement), and (3) the terms of the provided protection (e.g., whether the per-share value for the protected class will be determined (a) pursuant to a structured formula, such as one that references the new acquisition indebtedness without actually being tied to it, or (b) without regard to the entirety of the new acquisition indebtedness, but only to the extent necessary to make the post-transaction per-share value at least equal to the per-share transaction price).[2]

As a second valuation concern, it may be appropriate for each company to protect its shareholders by having its own financial advisor. Moreover, if (as described below) the transaction is structured so that an ESOP will exist at each company (even if momentarily), separate trustees and a financial advisor for each ESOP trustee will be *legally required.*[3] While multiple financial advisors can add to a transaction's cost, they may be required depending on the structure, and even if not required, having them may provide the parties (e.g., each company's board of directors) with a requisite degree of comfort.

Use of Retirement Plan and Certain IRA Assets as Transaction Consideration

It is possible, with proper safeguards and adequate disclosure, to use money transferred to the ESOP from a qualified retirement plan (in-

---

2. On a related note, in General Legal Advice Memo 2019-3, the IRS stated that price protection payments made by the sponsoring company directly to the employee are immediately taxable (whereas such payments are not immediately taxable if the company makes a special "qualified elective contribution" to the plan that is allocated to the employee's account and then distributed as part of the eventual distribution of the account).
3. See below under "When Section 1042 Treatment is Desired by Target Shareholders: Structure."

cluding qualified plan-based IRA dollars transferred into and then from a qualified plan) as consideration in an ESOP acquisition (with any monies rolling into the ESOP from these sources being viewed by senior lender(s) as transaction equity). To the extent that non-*employer* monies will be rolled over to aid in transaction financing, it must be decided how long the rollover opportunity will be extended to plan participants. Federal and state securities laws will also need to be examined for the level of required participant disclosure. Assuming that the amount of *employee* dollars being rolled over comes within federal and state securities law exemption parameters, a registration statement will not be required. However, even if a registration statement *is not required*, at a minimum, an information statement must be prepared to address applicable fraud concerns. Note that while the use of target plan (and/or IRA) monies for transaction financing can often add to the cost and complexity of a transaction, this use does serve to reduce otherwise-required transaction leverage while at the same time providing both an immediate allocation of shares and an immediate company stake to participants directing rollovers. While this structure is possible, it is very rarely used because of the cost and complexity involved.

Use of What Had Been Matching Contributions to Repay Acquisition Indebtedness

Another general consideration when using ESOPs in mergers and acquisitions is whether the company will use what *had been* matching contributions to its 401(k) plan to repay ESOP acquisition indebtedness. Some companies will leave prior 401(k) cash matching provisions unchanged, and others will not. Continuing 401(k) matching contributions while making ESOP contributions required to service an ESOP loan may result in unintended (and, perhaps, above-market and/or greater-than-base compensation) employee benefit levels. To the extent that such a result does not occur and/or a decision is made to still use what had been cash-matching contributions to repay ESOP acquisition indebtedness, a match corresponding to 401(k) salary reduction contributions can, if desired, still be made—and it can be made without additional dollars. A provision can be drafted in the ESOP plan to provide that, instead of allocating suspense account shares under the ESOP in one step (i.e., generally pro rata based on compensation), suspense account shares will be allocated in a two-step process. First, subject to discrimination testing, an amount of the suspense account shares to be released for the year will be allocated to ESOP participants so as to provide them with a desired benefit level corresponding to a specified percentage of the salary-reduction contributions made under the company's 401(k) plan. The remaining suspense account shares released for the year can then be allocated under the ESOP in a second step—generally, pro rata based on compensation.

(Editor's note: Based on conversations with companies that have made acquisitions, the NCEO has found that a reduction in 401(k) contributions by the acquiring company as part of the acquisition financing is rare. A post-acquisition issue in all cases is how to integrate the existing benefit plan structure at the target company into the acquiring company's benefit plan structure. This may involve some adjustment to the existing benefit levels in target companies. This issue must be handled very carefully because any significant reduction in benefit levels for target company employees could cause significant employee engagement issues and possibly lead to increased turnover.)

When Section 1042 Treatment Is Desired by Target Shareholders

Advantages

Once a company has adopted a leveraged ESOP, using an ESOP structure to acquire a target company can have significant advantages. First, to the extent that a target shareholder is able to sell their company shares to an ESOP and make a Section 1042[4] tax-deferred/tax-free election, the shareholder may be willing to pass on part of their income tax savings in the form of a reduced purchase price.

4. All section references in this chapter are to the Internal Revenue Code.

Second, to the extent that IRA and 401(k) dollars are rolled into the ESOP by target company employees, the amount of "outside funds" needed to acquire the target is reduced.

A third advantage is that the target company's seller may be willing to take a note in payment for the company rather than receiving cash up front. In this structure, the seller would sell stock to the ESOP in the target company in exchange for a note. The target company's ESOP would be merged into the acquiring company's ESOP. The terms of the note may provide the seller with certain control rights or covenants over how cash is used to make sure that the note is paid off. The seller would receive an interest rate based on rates for subordinated debt, providing a higher rate of return than would be available, for instance, if the seller took the proceeds from a sale and invested them in treasury bonds. In addition, as is true in almost all ESOP purchase transactions, the transaction's timing can be easily controlled, and the transaction's occurrence can remain totally confidential (e.g., from the target's customers) until the closing of the transaction.

From the *acquirer's* viewpoint, in a C corporation context, both the interest and principal on the related acquisition indebtedness will be effectively tax-deductible. In an S corporation context, it may be possible to acquire a target as a subsidiary of the acquirer and then make a qualified subchapter S subsidiary (QSub) election so that the target's income will flow up to the acquirer (with the acquirer's income being exempt from federal, and in many cases, state, income tax to the extent it is owned by an ESOP).

Disadvantages

The principal *disadvantage* of using an ESOP to acquire another company is that the transaction structure (as described immediately below) is generally more complicated and may be more costly than a typical asset or stock acquisition structure. A second disadvantage is that the per-share price of the acquirer's ESOP stock value may decrease after the transaction for two reasons. First, as described above, using the acquirer's existing cash in the acquisition, either by itself or when coupled with other factors (e.g., grants of stock-based compensation), may lower the per-share value of the company's shares on a post-transaction basis. Second, to the extent that the transaction is structured using the two-step ESOP-merger structure described below, the *per-share* value of the acquirer's stock may decrease due to the increase in the number of outstanding shares following the merger of the two ESOP plans.[5] Assuming the transaction is successful, however, these valuation impacts will be short-term, and the acquisition will add to the long-term value of the acquiring company.

Structure

Exchange Structure

If the acquirer is a C corporation, some practitioners believe that the owner of the target shares can simply exchange their shares for shares of the acquirer and then sell the received acquirer shares to the acquirer's ESOP (with the former target shareholder thereafter making a Section 1042 election). Because the exchange of shares will be designed to constitute a tax-free reorganization, transaction advisors will have to determine that the tax-free nature of the exchange will not be undermined by an immediate sale of the received shares to the acquirer's ESOP. This will depend in large part on whether the advisors can determine that required reorganization "continuity" is not "busted" by the subsequent sale to the ESOP (with some practitioners believing that continuity still remains since shares are not being sold to the acquirer or a corporation related to the acquirer).[6]

Merger Structure

If the acquirer is an S corporation (or a C corporation with advisors who believe that continuity will be broken by a post-exchange sale to an

---

5. Whether the increase in the number of outstanding shares will cause the per-share value of the acquirer to so drop will depend in great part on whether the target is acquired at a stock exchange rate that reflects the drop in the target's value resulting from the debt.
6. In this regard, see the continuity of interest regulations at Treas. Reg. § 1.368-1(e). See also PLRs 20100528 and 200052023.

ESOP), the transaction will likely be structured so that an ESOP that is substantially identical to the acquirer's ESOP is adopted by the target to purchase shares of the target shareholder(s). Once target shareholders sell their shares to the target ESOP, with the target ESOP usually using one or more ESOP notes for its consideration, the target will generally be merged into the acquirer or an acquirer subsidiary, with the ESOP notes received by the target shareholders often being "cashed out" in the merger.[7] The target's ESOP will then be merged into the acquirer's ESOP (with the acquirer assuming the debt obligations of the target ESOP).

Repayment of the acquisition indebtedness will generally occur via the company's cash flow, together with:

1. dollars the target might have annually contributed as a match to its 401(k) plan, with the acquirer, again, having the ability (if desired) to continue under the ESOP any prior 401(k) "match" made by the target and/or the acquirer (with the match, again, being made within the ESOP in the form of company shares), and/or
2. dollars saved due to or because of either (a) ESOP-generated income tax deductions (in a C corporation context) or (b) the ESOP's ownership percentage that goes untaxed in an S corporation.

Administrative and Other Considerations

To the extent that the target is a C corporation that will merge into an S corporation acquirer (or an acquirer QSub), target stock classes other than common will have to be converted into common before or as a part of the merger. Similarly, any target share class that has voting rights different than those in the S corporation acquirer will have to be converted before or as a part of the merger (because an S corporation can hold only voting and non-voting common shares). Assuming that the target class(es) is/are so converted, a C corporation that merges into an S corporation acquirer (or an acquirer subsidiary) will not be required to pay its own federal income taxes. Because the subsidiary

7. Note that the cashing out of the ESOP note(s) so received is not an essential step; should the acquirer want to, it can pay the note(s) over time (e.g., through the ESOP), if that is the deal.

will be wholly owned by the S corporation, the parent can make a QSub election under Section 1361(b)(3) that will treat the subsidiary as a disregarded entity, legally merging its tax identity into the parent S corporation. Since S corporations owned by an ESOP effectively pay zero federal income taxes, the subsidiary will not owe separate taxes.[8]

To the extent that the acquirer is a C (rather than an S) corporation, an existing multi-class stock structure within either the acquirer or the target may have to be considered when merging the target into the acquirer. In addition, because C corporation ESOP loans generally are shorter than their S corporation counterparts (to generate larger deductions that are unnecessary in a 100% S corporation ESOP structure), tracking on a loan-by-loan basis will be required for both the dividend deduction rule of Section 404(k) and the distribution delay rule under Section 409(o)(1)(B), which allows non-death and non-retirement distributions to be delayed until the ESOP loan is repaid.

Finally, the share exchange ratio that is applicable in the merger will be the subject of much debate between the respective ESOP trustees and their advisors. For purposes of the exchange, the target may be given quite a low post-ESOP purchase value due to target company obligations on the ESOP note(s) given to the target shareholders. If this is the case, from a financial fairness viewpoint, the target financial advisors may balk at the small number of acquirer shares slated for receipt by target ESOP participants in the merger. If the target is given an equal or *higher* post-ESOP purchase value (with target participants thus slated to receive a *higher* number of shares in the merger), the acquirer will have essentially paid twice for the target: first, by cashing out the target shareholder ESOP note(s) (as a part of the merger), and

---

8. Note that, while exempt from Federal taxation, certain states (like California) impose an entity-level franchise tax or minimum fee on S corporations. Note also that, because the subsidiary originated as a C corporation, the S corporation parent may be subject to a corporate-level tax on built-in gains if the subsidiary's assets are sold or disposed within five years of the QSub election. As to the election, it is highly recommended that it be in place effective upon the exact date the drop-down subsidiary is formed, which is before the merger. If the parent S corporation creates a brand-new subsidiary specifically to act as the merger vehicle, making the QSub election effective on the date of inception prevents the subsidiary from ever existing as a separate taxable entity.

second, by delivering a not-insignificant amount of acquirer shares in the merger (thereby diluting existing acquirer ESOP participants).

When Section 1042 Treatment Is Not Desired by Target Shareholders

Stock Purchase

Structure

If the acquirer is an S corporation owned wholly by an ESOP, it will not be concerned with deductions. In that case, the target seller can simply sell their shares to the acquirer or an acquirer subsidiary. If, on the other hand, the acquirer is a C corporation owned wholly or partially by an ESOP, deductions will be important. In that case, the transaction may be structured so that target shareholders sell their shares to an ESOP, even if they are not interested in making Section 1042 elections (so that the acquirer-controlled group will have maximized the deductions available to it). Depending upon the view of transaction advisors as to continuity (as discussed above), the target shareholders will either exchange their shares for shares of the acquirer and sell to the acquirer's ESOP or sell their shares to a newly adopted target ESOP (with the target thereafter merging into the acquirer and the target ESOP thereafter merging into the acquirer's ESOP).

Advantages

If the target shareholder sells shares directly to the acquirer rather than to an ESOP, the advantage will be that Section 404 and Section 415 contribution and allocation limits will never become an issue in terms of paying back the acquisition indebtedness. If a target shareholder instead sells shares to an ESOP, all of the normal ESOP advantages will be available. The seller will be able to sell stock rather than assets, which may be preferable in terms of distancing the seller from existing target liabilities. The seller will also receive cash and/or notes rather than shares of another company (as might occur in a typical merger structure). Because the seller will sell shares (rather than assets), the seller will also have a single level of taxation. In addition, because the shares are being sold to an ESOP, the seller will receive capital gains treatment on *all* of their sales proceeds, engage (if desired) in a totally confidential transaction, have ESOP-related advantageous seller financing (other than the tax-free receipt of principal), and *not* be asked to take a "haircut" on the price (as they might be asked if shares were being sold to the ESOP in a Section 1042 transaction).

From the acquisition company's viewpoint, if the target seller simply sells their shares to the acquisition company, both the seller and the acquirer will experience a less complex transaction, and the acquirer will not have to deal with Section 404 and 415 combined plan limits on a post-transaction basis. If, on the other hand, a target shareholder sells to an ESOP (but without making a Section 1042 election), the transaction structure will allow for the use of ESOP rollovers to reduce the amount of transaction-required financing, the use of what had previously been 401(k) matching payments to repay transaction financing, and the deductibility of both interest *and* principal. The extent to which there is a concern with maximizing the acquirer group's deductions will likely turn on whether the acquirer is operating under an S corporation election.

Disadvantages

The principal disadvantage of a target shareholder selling shares but not making a Section 1042 election is that, from the acquirer's viewpoint, the seller has no incentive to take a haircut on their sale price. Similarly, seller financing will not be as attractive to the seller because—without the seller making a Section 1042 election—the transaction cannot be structured so that the seller receives seller-financing principal payments tax-free. To the extent that the target seller instead sells shares directly to the acquirer (rather than to an ESOP), principal payments on the acquisition indebtedness will not be effectively deductible. Moreover, if the acquirer is an S corporation, the seller will be assured that *all* of their gain will be characterized as a capital gain (as would be the case if they were to sell shares to an ESOP) *only if* the seller refuses to make a Section 338(h)(10) (asset sale treatment) election.

Administrative (and Other) Considerations

If the target shareholder sells to an ESOP but *does not* make an election under Section 1042, the administrative (and other) considerations described above under "When Section 1042 Treatment Is Desired by Target Shareholders" will apply.

Asset Purchase

Structure

There may be instances where, for liability, tax, and/or other reasons, the acquirer may want assets purchased rather than stock. Normally, the acquirer would simply purchase assets for itself (i.e., *outside* the context of its ESOP). If, however, all of the acquirer's shares were owned by an ESOP and the acquirer wanted to flow the acquisition indebtedness through the ESOP, an asset purchase structure might be designed in a very limited circumstance to have the acquirer sell treasury shares to the acquirer's ESOP and then use the received sale proceeds to purchase all or a portion of the target's ESOP.[9] If the acquirer's ESOP *does not* own 100% of the acquirer's stock, such a structure would likely not be employed since its use would dilute any existing non-ESOP shareholders. In such a case, the target's assets would be sold directly to the acquirer.

Advantages

The principal advantage of an asset sale to the seller is that the seller may be able to get a higher purchase price if the acquirer is a tax-paying C corporation. The reason is that the acquirer will be able to depreciate the purchased assets from their transaction-date fair market value (thereby increasing the acquirer's deductions). If all of

9. This might occur, for example, if (1) the acquirer was a C corporation that was not about to become an S corporation, (2) the acquirer was in need of deductions, (3) it had no outside synthetic equity holders, and (4) it was concerned about moving more ESOP allocations to its newer employees (e.g., in a "have and have-nots" scenario).

the acquirer's shares are owned by an ESOP, the acquirer's deductions can be even further increased in such a case if its ability to depreciate the purchased assets at their closing date fair market value is financed by the acquirer's use of treasury share sale proceeds (with the ESOP loan undertaken to permit the ESOP's purchase of treasury shares effectively allowing the acquirer to deduct acquisition indebtedness principal payments).[10]

Of course, to the extent that the acquirer is an S corporation that is wholly owned by an ESOP, deductions will be important to the acquirer group only to the extent they can be taken on applicable state tax returns. In such a case, the principal advantage of an asset purchase structure is that the acquirer may feel that it is acquiring fewer liabilities than it would were it purchasing the target's stock. (Whether this would actually be true would depend on the parties' relative bargaining powers in terms of purchase agreement representation and warranty and indemnification provisions.)

Disadvantages

Again, to the extent that either the acquirer's ESOP does not own 100% of the acquirer's stock or synthetic equity exists outside the ESOP, a structure involving an ESOP's purchase of acquirer treasury shares would be disadvantageous in terms of dilution to non-ESOP acquirer shareholders. From the *seller's* viewpoint, to the extent that assets rather than shares are sold, the seller will have two levels of taxation if the seller was formerly a C corporation and is within the five-year built-in gain (BIG) recognition period (with the first level of taxation (the "BIG tax") being triggered by the target selling the assets and the second level being triggered by the target being liquidated). A sale of the target's assets rather than its stock will mean that the target's

10. Such additional deductions may not be important if the acquirer can make an election to be taxed as an S corporation. There may, however, be considerations (e.g., desired retention of multiple classes of stock) which make an S corporation election impractical. In addition, even if an S corporation election will be made by a 100% ESOP-owned acquirer, state tax law considerations may make additional deductions desirable.

contracts will have to be novated, which may not be required if target shares (rather than target assets) are sold.

Administrative (and Other) Considerations

The administrative and other concerns will be similar to those described above under "When Section 1042 Treatment Is Desired by Target Shareholders," including the possibility of having to track loans and/or dividends.

Acquisition Fiduciary and Settlor Issues

In every acquisition involving one or more ESOPs, normal ESOP acquisition-related fiduciary and settlor issues will arise. The transaction fiduciary will want to assure itself that the company's board is doing its job, and it may be concerned about the possible applicability of a "protected (floor) price" for ESOP shares received by participants before the date that new transaction indebtedness is repaid (as discussed above under "Valuation Concerns"). Examples of settlor issues that may arise include (1) an analysis as to whether the target's plans should be amended, terminated, or merged into the acquirer's plans (as discussed above under "Continuation, Termination, or Possible Merger of Existing Target Plans"), and (2) decisions as to whether and when target employees will be brought into the acquirer's ESOP (also discussed above under "Continuation, Termination, or Possible Merger of Existing Target Plans").

Acquisition Corporate Governance Issues

Corporate governance issues that arise in acquisitions include the role of the board versus the role of plan fiduciaries and the participant voting process[11] (taking into account concerns regarding possible required pass-through votes and/or rules with regard to shareholder consent).

11. There will be a need for a participant vote at the target level if the target has an ESOP and the target will either be merging with the acquirer or selling substantially all of its assets. There will also be a need for a voting pass-through

Both the US Department of Labor (DOL) and the plaintiffs' bar could challenge ESOP acquisition transactions. Challenges specifically to ESOP acquisitions of unrelated third-party targets have to date been comparatively uncommon, but both DOL and private plaintiffs have litigated ESOP formation and initial-purchase (overpayment) transactions extensively, and the documentation guidance set forth here should be read against that active enforcement and litigation environment.

In the past, there was guidance suggesting that both board of directors and ESOP fiduciary meeting minutes should reflect only what was accomplished at the meeting (e.g., a vote) and not the considerations that were vetted before the resulting action(s) occurred. In the current ESOP litigation environment, this guidance has changed dramatically. In documenting an ESOP transaction, it is critically important that both board and trustee minutes reflect the discussion of the various benefits, drawbacks, and considerations that were part of any decision to proceed with the subject ESOP transaction. These minutes should reflect careful consideration and discussion of all valuation, financing, and fairness issues.

Acquisition Financing Concerns

Acquisition financing concerns include the added tax advantages of the ESOP term loan and ESOP-related seller financing, which will not be present if conventional financing is used to finance the acquisition of a target. Where an ESOP purchase is included in the acquisition structure, financing-related issues will include (1) a determination of how long the term a new ESOP acquisition indebtedness should be (in terms of its impact on an existing ESOP benefit level; desired deductions, if any; and applicable contribution, dividend, and deduction limitations), (2) the impact of the acquisition on existing ESOP repurchase obligations, (3) whether participants should be given an opportunity to roll dollars into the ESOP so as to "whittle down" the

at the acquirer level in the case of a merger unless the merger is designed as a triangular merger (i.e., a merger with a subsidiary of the acquirer rather than the acquirer itself).

required amount of ESOP acquisition indebtedness, and (4) whether matching dollars that had previously been contributed to a 401(k) plan should be used to repay ESOP indebtedness (with the match moving inside the ESOP as described above under "Use of What Had Been Matching Contributions to Repay Acquisition Indebtedness").

Conclusion

Using an ESOP purchase structure may be advantageous in that a seller who can make a Section 1042 election may be willing to pass part of the seller's tax savings on to the acquirer in the form of a reduced purchase price. However, even if the seller does not make a Section 1042 election, an ESOP purchase structure can permit the acquirer to purchase shares with pretax dollars, and it can allow for accessing other qualified plan and IRA monies to reduce the acquisition indebtedness. Monies that would otherwise be contributed as a 401(k) match can also be used under an ESOP purchase structure to provide a partial funding source for periodic loan payments. Coupling these advantages with how ESOP financing enhances cash flow (which can be used for both debt reduction and periodic growth) may, in fact, make the ESOP structure a worthy alternative to traditional M&A acquisition structures in many situations. An ESOP purchase structure can also serve as a go-forward investment and/or acquisition platform. Finally, the use of an ESOP as a stalking horse and/or acquisition tool may also provide an acquirer or an M&A firm with advantage(s) not found elsewhere.

With proper planning, the considerations that must be explored and quantified in any ESOP structure need not be structural drawbacks. In an economy where M&A advisors and private equity groups are looking for flexible structures to take acquisitions to completion, the leveraged ESOP purchase structure presents a compelling alternative. Although beyond the scope of this chapter, the structure's use may also make an ESOP an appropriate acquisition vehicle in the case of a desired divestiture (including a spinoff of a division or company, e.g., a failed "roll-up" company) and/or a private equity group that is seeking to liquidate its equity investment in a "sideways" company.

CHAPTER 4

Should a Company Acquire or Merge with an ESOP Company?

John Burgess

IN MOST CASES when ESOP companies buy other companies, the sale is structured as an acquisition; in some cases, however, there are benefits to merging instead. So which is better? To answer this question, it is helpful to understand the various ways corporate acquisitions occur. Generally, acquisitions can fall into one of three approaches: an asset acquisition of the target, a stock acquisition of the target, or a merger of the target into the acquiring company.

Chapter 3 explores in detail the ways transactions can be structured and their tax consequences for buyers and sellers. This chapter takes a narrower focus on the pros and cons of mergers versus acquisitions.

An asset acquisition is the purchase of the target's business assets without acquiring ownership of the target entity. If the target company retains its prior ownership, it will typically liquidate as soon as practicable after receipt of all of the transaction consideration, including earnouts and escrows, because all of its business assets were purchased. In most cases, liabilities of the target are left behind, with the funds from the asset purchase used by the target to pay them.

In a stock acquisition, the buyer acquires the ownership of the target company, with the target maintaining a separate legal existence and usually becoming a subsidiary of the buyer after the transaction closes.

In a merger, the target company is absorbed by the acquiring company, thereby ending its existence. Usually, the acquiring company will continue in existence as before, but in some cases, an entirely new corporation is formed and is the final entity remaining after the merger.

Which one is best depends on the circumstances. For the most part, the same considerations that apply to acquisitions by non-ESOP companies also apply to those by ESOP companies, although, naturally, the ESOP introduces some nuances. In the non-ESOP world, tax consequences are a big driver of which approach is best for a given acquisition. For acquisitions by ESOP companies, that might not be as big a concern, especially where the buyer is a 100% ESOP-owned S corporation that doesn't have to worry about federal income taxes. However, tax consequences cannot be completely ignored, and because every company's situation is different (including state and local tax issues), the help of a good CPA firm is crucial.

The other consideration that is unique to acquiring an ESOP company is that a merger is more conducive to the target company's ESOP continuing after the transaction, typically after a merger into the acquiring company's ESOP. With stock and asset acquisitions, the target's ESOP is nearly always terminated and liquidated. That can result in large payouts to participants (which can be rolled over on a tax-deferred basis), but if the payouts are big enough, they could lead to many employees leaving the workforce, disrupting the business.

Some of the main advantages and disadvantages of each of the flavors of acquisitions follow.

Asset Acquisitions

As mentioned above, the main advantage to a buyer in an asset acquisition is that the buyer generally does not become responsible for the liabilities of the entity that it purchases unless the buyer agrees to assume certain liabilities listed in the purchase agreement.

Asset acquisitions also do not require all shareholders to consent to the acquisition, although the transaction must be approved by a percentage of shareholders specified in state law, typically those representing a majority of the shares. However, a company can increase this threshold through either its articles of incorporation, its bylaws, or a shareholder agreement. Assuming that the target has not made some sort of agreement to require approval from all shareholders, a few small minority shareholders will not be able to hold up the transaction, which could happen in a stock acquisition if certain protections are not already in place.

There are some downsides to an asset acquisition. First, none of the key contracts that the target company has will automatically be transferred to the buyer. In many cases, a contract will require consent from the other party for it to be transferred from the seller to the buyer. If the contracts are important to the business and difficult or time-consuming to transfer (for example, government contracts), the process of doing that might make a stock purchase better. And even when the other party does not have an issue with transferring the contract to the buyer, it does give the other party some leverage in renegotiating some terms to be more favorable to it in exchange for consent to make the transfer. But the flip side of this is that the buyer does not have to assume any contracts that the seller had (barring some language in the contract that says otherwise), so where there is a contract that has become unfavorable to the seller, it may be possible to renegotiate something more favorable to the buyer going forward. The same thing is true if the business holds any licenses that are required for it to operate, if the purchaser does not have that license.

Asset acquisitions can also be disruptive to employees. First, the ones who are going to continue to work in the business will have to be rehired and onboarded by the purchaser. Their pay and benefits are subject to change, although in some cases, the asset purchase agreement requires the buyer to continue their pay and benefits at certain levels for a period after the transaction closes.

Major assets such as real estate and vehicles, if they are purchased in an asset acquisition, will need to be retitled in the name of the buyer.

This is not particularly difficult, but it means that more paperwork and likely more transfer taxes will need to be addressed.

If the target is an ESOP company, there will need to be a pass-through vote in which participants will be able to vote any stock that is allocated to their accounts. The ESOP trustee votes unallocated shares and the shares of any participants who do not send back a vote. Because the transaction usually involves a significant premium above the most recent fair market value, participants tend to overwhelmingly vote in favor of the transaction. However, this does require a disclosure statement to be provided to participants in which the material terms of the transaction will need to be described, and the voting process will require two to three more weeks to be built into the timeline for closing. Plus, participants will necessarily be made aware of the transaction before it closes, which may or may not be desirable.

Stock Acquisitions

When the buyer simply purchases the outstanding stock of the target, everything in the business of the target—assets, liabilities, and everything else—goes to the buyer in the transaction. The entity continues in existence, so employees can continue their current employment relationship (and again, a purchase agreement can require the buyer to maintain a certain level of pay and benefits for some time).

Contracts and licenses do not need to be assigned or transferred, although some contracts may have a change-in-control provision that requires the other party to the transaction to consent to the contract continuing due to the new ownership. Licenses should also be reviewed to make sure that the change in ownership of the company does not affect their status.

In a stock acquisition, buyers typically are not willing to go through with the transaction unless they can purchase 100% of the target company. In the absence of a buy-sell agreement or shareholder agreement that would require minority shareholders to go along with the majority in the sale (sometimes called a "drag-along" provision), small shareholders have the ability to hold out. In addition to causing headaches, this could increase the cost of the transaction to the buyer.

A pass-through vote by the ESOP shareholders is not required if the transaction is simply a straight stock purchase. Some ESOP companies will conduct a pass-through vote anyway, which may be done as another way to make employees feel like true owners of the company, in the same way that some companies will let employees vote shares on routine corporate issues when a pass-through vote is not legally required. It should be confirmed that a plan document or trust agreement of the target is not written to require a pass-through vote in a stock sale.

One more twist: What if you're buying the stock or membership interests of a subsidiary of an ESOP company, but not the stock of the ESOP sponsor itself? That's an asset acquisition, and depending on the size of the subsidiary relative to the overall business under the ESOP sponsor, that might require a pass-through vote. Transactions are sometimes structured this way for tax purposes.

Mergers

In a corporate merger, the target company is absorbed into the buyer or a subsidiary corporation of the buyer that is formed to facilitate the merger (in some cases, a new corporation can be formed to absorb both entities, but this discussion assumes the buyer is the entity in place going forward). Mergers can be especially useful where the selling shareholders want to maintain ownership in the continuing entity, and mergers can be structured to defer or minimize taxes for the sellers. If structured properly, a merger of two corporations can result in a deferral of capital gains taxes to the shareholders of the target company to the extent that the merger consideration consists of stock of the acquiring entity. Some of the deal consideration can be paid in cash, but the shareholders would be taxed immediately on that portion of the consideration. There are several ways to accomplish a corporate merger to achieve the tax and legal consequences desired by the parties.

In a legal sense, a merger results in a mix of the advantages and disadvantages of asset deals and stock deals. As in a stock sale, all of the target's assets and liabilities automatically transfer to the buyer, but since the prior owner is no longer in existence, it is necessary to retitle assets like real estate and vehicles. Contracts and licenses are also automatically transferred over to the buyer, absent a requirement in the contract that the other party approves the transfer of the contract, or other requirements that might restrict a transfer of the license. The employment of employees is also automatically assumed by the buyer, although they will have a new employer name on their paychecks.

As with an asset sale, unanimous shareholder approval is typically not required for a merger, absent any corporate governing documents to the contrary. Where ESOPs are involved, however, mergers do require a pass-through vote, regardless of whether the ESOP company is the one doing the acquisition or being acquired. So if two ESOP companies are involved in the merger, then participants in both companies will have to be given the chance to vote.

Where two ESOP companies are involved in a merger, one of the main attractions is that the companies can merge their ESOPs into one plan as part of the acquisition. This is a complex process with lots of parties involved, but it might be the best solution and should at least be considered where one ESOP company is acquiring another.

One of the ESOPs, typically the one sponsored by the acquiring company, will need to be designated as the surviving ESOP after the merger. The shares of the target company that are held in the ESOP are exchanged for shares of the acquiring company, so that there is one plan for all participants holding stock of the acquiring company.

Chapter 3 discusses these considerations in more detail.

CHAPTER 5

Issues for ESOP Companies Acquiring Other ESOP Companies

Corey Rosen

MORE AND MORE, ESOP companies are acquiring other ESOP companies. Such acquisitions can be appealing because the most difficult challenge of an acquisition is integration, including operational integration but especially cultural integration, and two ESOP companies are more likely to begin with at least similar cultures.

This chapter begins by examining what research tells us about what makes mergers and acquisitions succeed or fail, which applies equally well to any acquisition or merger. The following sections look at valuation issues, issues concerning merging two plans with different rules and at different stages of development, communication concerns, cultural and operational integration, and compensation issues. Finally, an appendix provides sample questionnaires for those involved in the merger or acquisition to assess how it is working. This chapter partly draws from material generously provided to the NCEO by the Boston Consulting Group.

Factors That Cause Mergers to Succeed or Fail

The success or failure of a merger depends on how the terms are defined. At the extreme, the acquired company ends up shrinking substantially or closing altogether, or the acquiring company suffers significant financial loss due to the transaction. However, many business leaders would say that if the acquisition or merger does not produce the kinds of results that the deal was premised on, that also constitutes failure. The acquiring firm might find that it ends up spending far more time on making the deal work than expected, that the cultures clash and key people leave, that expected cost synergies do not materialize, that combined profits are below what would be required to fully justify the price paid, or that in some other way, one company or both wishes they had never met one another.

Business psychology makes it almost inevitable that many mergers and acquisitions will fail. One of psychology's most confirmed findings is the optimism bias. For instance, people tend to think they have much less risk for disease and crime than they really do and think they are much more likely to succeed in their fields or financially than they really will. In fact, depressed people have the most accurate projections (which may be why there is an optimism bias—it is too discouraging to go through life without one). Company leaders are particularly prone to optimism bias because they tend to be much more self-confident. That means that company leaders making acquisitions are likely to overestimate the chances of success, as research consistently shows. A key element in assessing any merger or acquisition, then, is to go in with very conservative expectations. If possible, having neutral third parties help assess how likely success will be and what obstacles might arise can be very helpful.

Most mergers, at least in the public company sector, do not live up to expectations. According to the Boston Consulting Group, of 277 mergers between 1985 and 2000, 56% destroyed value rather than created it. Booz Allen was even more pessimistic, saying that only one-third of mergers added value, while many struggled or failed.

In looking at what makes mergers and acquisitions work, several key steps are needed:[1]

1. *Determine whether the goal of the merger is to consolidate and save costs or to grow and acquire new capacity by gaining new technologies and/or markets.*

If the goal is consolidation, integration needs to move quickly. Generally, if there are going to be cost savings, if they do not show up in the first 12 to 18 months, these kinds of mergers are not likely to succeed. That means that there should be highly directive, top-down leadership. It is not a merger of equals. Ideally, a team is assigned to identify where the cost savings will come from. Of course, these strategies come at a cost. There is likely to be a significant decline in morale and possibly an increase in voluntary turnover in the target (or in a merger, the areas where the cost-cutting occurs), including key people. That can mean that any cost savings generated may be quickly overwhelmed by losses in long-term performance. This is part of why acquisitions have such a low rate of success. In the NCEO's view, ESOP companies generally do not benefit from these acquisitions because they create two cultures that are very different and possibly antagonistic. ESOP acquisitions or mergers are much more common when there are perceived complementarities in products, technology, or marketing, such as when one company can help expand a market, add a needed technological capacity, or diversify product lines. Most ESOP acquisitions are of the first sort. Based on a tabulation of ESOP acquisitions reported in the press over the last several years, it appears about 80% were of companies where the acquirer purchased a company doing the same thing but in a different market with a goal of expanding its operations. We have seen growth in recent years, however, of ESOP holding companies, some of which have the explicit goal of diversification. Regardless of the reasons for acquisitions or mergers, ESOP companies rarely pursue companies when they plan to reduce the workforce.

In a growth transaction, the company being absorbed (or the two companies forming a combination of equals) can proceed at a more

1. Part of the material in the first section of this chapter is based on a presentation on this topic from the Boston Consulting Group.

deliberate pace than in a consolidation transaction. Teams of people from both companies need to be established to evaluate a variety of integration issues, such as technology systems, enterprise management software, benefit program integration, strategic planning, training systems, internal and public websites, marketing programs and brand identity, and employee communications and involvement systems. At the management level, a central team needs to coordinate these efforts.

2. Monitor employee reactions to the merger.

This can be done by surveys, focus groups, websites to post comments and questions (perhaps anonymously), etc. Focus groups, for instance, can be used to identify differences in "the way we do things here." That does not mean, however, that different approaches are necessarily problematic. If two companies with effective cultures and systems merge, it may well be that the ideal outcome is for both companies to retain those elements that make their company work especially well, with each company learning from the other how what one company does may provide useful tools for the other.

3. Do not overlook customers and suppliers in the merger process.

How will they view the merger? If the units have largely separate markets, this may not be an issue, but if the markets are similar, it may make sense to set up a group to talk with customers about what is happening, see what concerns they have, and perhaps pick up any ideas for new opportunities. In fact, this may be a very good time for salespeople to start finding out what else customers need that they can now provide with the new capacity. If the merged companies provide a larger market for suppliers, this may also be an opportunity to reduce costs. For instance, with a larger volume of FedEx pickups, it may be possible to arrange a better cost structure with FedEx.

4. Decide how to handle strategic decisions.

Strategic decisions can be a particularly knotty issue. Local management will be accustomed to making these decisions. In a merged entity, even if the stated goal (as is often the case) is for each company to continue operating largely independently, the reality is that in almost every case, the more dominant party will want its strategic objectives to prevail when there is conflict. Rather than waiting for the inevitable, early on, leaders in both companies need to work out just how much freedom each company has and what kinds of decisions will be subject to an integrated decision-making process.

The appendix to this chapter provides questions, including ESOP-specific ones, to ask key players in the acquisition process to see whether the process is working.

Valuation of the Combined Entities

The valuation of the combined entities will proceed in much the same way as an ESOP valuation does. The appraiser looks at what a willing financial buyer would pay a willing seller, but now for the combined entity. The first task is to determine the enterprise value—the value of the company overall, as opposed to the value of individual shares.

The first key question is who now does the appraisal. Assuming each company is satisfied with its current appraiser, a decision needs to be made by the new board, subject to review by the new fiduciary, of who will do the appraisal going forward. The potential concern here is that appraisers use different techniques to value ESOPs and use different levels of aggressiveness in their assumptions. Hence, two very well-qualified appraisers are likely to differ on the value of any particular ESOP company. Generally, we at the NCEO have found that these variations are relatively small, in the 10% to 15% range, but if the two firms have appraisers with very different assumptions, there can be an issue, especially if one company has a particularly aggressive or conservative appraisal firm. While the range of difference may seem small given the uncertain art of appraisals, a difference of, say, 10% in one year may seem very consequential to ESOP participants. An essential element of the merger process is explaining openly and clearly why this has happened (if it does).

The chosen appraiser will focus primarily on some multiple of free cash flow, which usually accounts for 70% to 80% of the weighting in an ESOP appraisal, although that can differ in specific cases. The appraiser is essentially asking what a willing buyer would pay to gain access to these free cash flows, given the investment risk. The higher the perceived risk, the greater the return the investor will seek. In determining projected free cash flow, the appraiser may focus on projecting out from prior earnings, a technique used if earnings have been stable, or rely more heavily on management projections if (1) they are credible and (2) there is reason to think the future will be different from the past. A merger may affect these calculations not only for all the usual business reasons but also because one entity may be at a different stage of its ESOP debt repayment than another.

The remaining weight will be given to data from comparable company sales (if any), comparable public company valuations (if any), and asset value. The comparable company method usually receives limited weight because there are too many differences between ESOP companies and companies for which data can be obtained. Asset value is generally looked at for two reasons. If a company has a greater asset liquidation value than it is worth on an ongoing basis, then the asset value may be the primary determinant of value. That is not common in ESOP appraisals. But adjustments to the enterprise value derived from the free cash flow multiple approach may be made if the companies have assets that could be sold without affecting company operations or if significant debt or other liabilities may impede the company's future earnings potential.

Once an enterprise value has been determined, the appraiser needs to make adjustments for what shares in the ESOP are worth. In most ESOP acquisitions, the acquirer is a 100% ESOP-owned company, so control is not a factor. But if a minority ESOP-owned company buys another ESOP company, it is more complicated. The sale will be at a control price even if the target ESOP is a minority owner because all the shares are being sold at once. But the acquirer will still be valued at a non-control basis. Approaches to valuation take a very nuanced approach to control issues, but there will be some level of discount for a lack of strategic control.

An appraiser should also evaluate liquidity. The ESOP put option makes the shares more marketable than they would normally be in a closely held company, but the emerging repurchase obligation means the company may have a greater cash obligation for paying for its retirement benefits than it would if it did not have an ESOP. The appraiser should assess how great this difference is and adjust future earnings projections and share prices accordingly. This may result in changes in value of, typically, 5% to 15% over what would be the case absent this liability. The merger is likely to affect this calculation for a few reasons, although the ultimate impact may be fairly small (a few percentage points):

- The two companies are likely to be contributing different amounts to the ESOP each year.
- The two ESOPs may have differing amounts of cash in their plan available for repurchase.
- The two companies are likely to be at different stages of their ESOP and have differing demographics, numbers of shares vested, and, possibly, distribution and/or diversification schedules.
- The two companies may have different approaches to what happens to shares bought back from participants. When shares are bought back and retired, this has a different impact per share than when the shares are bought back by the ESOP or by the company and recontributed to the ESOP. When shares are retired, the enterprise value goes down, but so does the number of shares, so the impact is neutral per share. When shares are recontributed, there are more outstanding shares to be divided into enterprise value, but the recycled shares may be part of what the company would otherwise contribute to benefit plans and/or be a core part of the company's desire to retain employee ownership in the long term.

Protecting the Interests of Each Company's ESOP

First, some clarity is needed about what the transaction actually is. In a merger of equals, two firms, often of about the same size, agree to go forward as a single new company rather than remain separately owned and operated. Often, however, one company will buy another and call the transaction a merger of equals. In a pure merger, the two ESOPs would be combined, and the stock in each would be exchanged for new shares in the combined company. In an acquisition, the target ESOP would have its shares replaced by shares in the acquirer.

If the transaction is literally structured as a merger, participants in both ESOPs must be able to vote their allocated shares on it by directing the trustee. If it is technically an acquisition of assets, then the target employees must be able to vote their shares. If it is a share sale, there is no mandatory voting.

Trustees of the plans must determine whether the financial terms of the transaction are fair to both the ESOPs and their participants. Although that determination is ultimately the responsibility of the ESOP trustees, the boards of each company also have a fiduciary interest to protect shareholder interests, even if the only shareholder is the ESOP. To help ESOP fiduciaries make that determination, it is usually advisable for the trustee of each plan to obtain a fairness opinion. A single opinion is not advisable because the advisor would then be working for two different trustees who may have differing interests. Many companies also hire an independent transactional trustee for the deal if they use insiders. That will add some tens of thousands of dollars in costs, but it would also add expertise and a kind of insurance against later claims by the Department of Labor or plan participants because the courts generally regard this as a best practice.

In either case, plan fiduciaries (as well as boards) must assess whether what the participants in each plan will end up with is in their best interests. A fairness opinion is the best way to do that. It examines the terms and price of the transaction to determine whether the ESOP participants are getting a fair deal relative to other parties in the transaction. In an acquisition, the advisor looks at both whether the consideration paid for shares in the target company represents fair market value and whether it is fair relative to what the employees in the acquiring firm yield from the deal. In a merger, the issue is whether each ESOP is getting replacement shares that have the same value as the other ESOP, or one party is ending up with a better deal.

Reconciling Plan Differences

Differing plan rules can lead to tricky issues. Technically, it is possible to operate two different plans for each company, each with its own rules, but most companies want to create a single set of rules. Key plan rules include vesting, diversification, allocation, eligibility, plan entry dates, voting, and distribution. If the plans differ, one solution is to adopt the most liberal rule for each element for both plans. That will make participants happy but may raise financial or other issues for the combined company. If you pick and choose, certain considerations apply to each rule:

- *Eligibility:* You can change eligibility rules for future employees, but changing the rules to make it harder for an existing group of employees to qualify would likely cause legal problems and considerable morale issues.
- *Allocation:* Most plans use relative pay to allocate shares, but if the plans differ, you can change allocation rules going forward to have a common approach, provided they do meet the normal allocation requirements.
- *Vesting:* You cannot extend vesting requirements for currently allocated shares but can for future allocations.
- *Voting:* This is not a protected benefit, so if one company has full pass-through voting, it could be eliminated. This could create significant skepticism about the deal, however. At the NCEO, we have found that full voting rights have little if any effect on corporate governance, so extending full voting rights to the second company is unlikely to raise any issues.
- *Diversification:* If one plan provides for more liberal diversification rules than the other, and you want to keep that for these participants, you would need to extend that to the other participants as well.
- *Distributions:* This is where the difference may be largest and most significant. Anti-cutback rules limit how much you can change

distribution rules for existing participants (they can be changed for future ones). ESOP exceptions to these rules allow you to change the form of distribution from stock to cash or vice-versa and to change from immediate payout on distribution to installment payouts. There is no consensus on whether you can lengthen the time between termination and the start of distribution, however. So if one company starts distributions at three years and one after five, changing it all to five years could be a violation. While corporate counsel should advise on this, be aware that the change may have an adverse effect on motivation.

Aside from these rules, some companies have distribution policies hard-wired into the plan document and others in a separate written plan, so this needs to be synchronized. Some companies also may segregate accounts on termination by buying the shares for cash and investing the cash until a distribution event and/or use rebalancing programs that provide that cash and stock within the ESOP will be moved around each year so that each participant has the same percentage of stock and cash (this is often advised as a way to prevent having one group of owners and one of non-owners in mature ESOPs). These provisions are not subject to anti-cutback rules but need to be synchronized to avoid discrimination issues.

If there is a literal merger, most likely all the shares in each company are exchanged for shares in the new company. If it is technically an acquisition but called a merger, the target shares are exchanged for the acquiring company's shares.

The distribution of shares in a post-merger situation is usually a simple exchange. Assume, for instance, that company A's ESOP shares are worth 40% of the new company and company B's 60%. A new class of shares is set up with, for instance, a value of $50 per share with a total value of $10 million (meaning there are 20,000 shares). Each ESOP trustee exchanges all the shares in the respective ESOP trusts. Company A participants would get $4 million in shares (8,000 shares) and company B participants $6 million (12,000 shares). The per-share value in each existing ESOP, of course, would not be $50, but the exchange would be structured so that if an employee had $50,000 worth of stock before, they have $50,000 after, however many shares that turns out to be.

Other Employee Benefits and Compensation

Unless there are unions involved, each company normally retains its compensation structure for nonmanagement employees. Managers may now take on new duties, however, and their pay needs to be reevaluated.

A more difficult issue is the other benefits. One company may have a 401(k) plan with a match, and the other may have either no plan, a different match, or no match. Each company can retain its own plan, or a blended approach can be chosen. There is no protected right to any level of 401(k) contributions, and almost all plans provide immediate or very fast eligibility. Health plans may be trickier. Again, each company can maintain its own plan, but employees in the less beneficial plan may now wonder why their colleagues are getting a better deal (assuming they find out about it, which is likely).

Combining a Mature ESOP with a Young ESOP

A common operational challenge is the "have/have not" problem. Mature ESOPs have paid off their acquisition debt, while newer ESOPs may still be allocating shares. As employees join the mature ESOP company, the only shares being added each year might be those bought back either by the ESOP with cash in the trust or by the company, which would buy the shares and recontribute them to the ESOP (a more common and recommended approach because it provides more flexibility in annual contributions so that they can be roughly equal each year). If a mature company merges with a less mature one, the remaining acquisition debt is often paid off, so now all new employees will have this issue.

So how can new employees get shares? Sometimes (but not usually), the recycled shares are sufficient, but if not, rebalancing and account segregation are advisable. Rebalancing provides that if there is cash in the ESOP, each year, shares will be bought and sold so that all employees end up with the same percentage of each. For instance, say John has $10,000, all in cash, and Mary has $100,000, all in stock. Overall, 80% of plan assets are in company stock. The trustee would buy and sell shares within the trust so that John would now have $2,000 in cash and $8,000 in stock, and Mary would have $80,000 in stock and $20,000 in cash. Another common approach is "profit sharing" accounting, in which each employee ends up with the same percentage of shares and other investments as each other employee.

Account segregation provides that when people terminate, their shares are exchanged for cash investments until distribution. Both rebalancing and segregation assume the company is contributing cash to the plan each year after the acquisition debt is repaid.

In 2010, the IRS made it clear that account segregation and rebalancing are allowable, provided certain rules are met. The plan document must state that these tools are available and include the rules for them.

The IRS made several key points to keep in mind:

1. There must be a written program in the plan to set out a "definite predetermined allocation formula." That should include the number of shares (presumably a formula that will be applied each year to arrive at the number) and the manner in which the transfer will be effectuated, including the applicable valuation date.
2. The right of each participant to have a particular form of investment does not raise the issue of "effective availability of benefits" so long as all participants are treated in the same way. For segregation, because these participants are a separate employee class, nondiscriminatory reshuffling also does not affect current availability.
3. The right to retain employer stock is not a protected benefit. However, the rebalancing cannot be done in such a way that someone who has diversified their account into cash now will have some of that cash moved back into stock.

Communicating the Transaction

Until the deal is complete, or if employees have to vote on it, the merger discussions should be strictly confidential. Once these points have been reached, it is essential to aggressively communicate about what is going on. I suggest several key strategies:

- Set up a joint communication team with people from both companies. Ideally, this would consist of both managers and some nonmanagement employees from existing ESOP communications committees (if you do not have one, now is a good time to start).
- Have an "all-hands" meeting to explain the merger. Make sure that you describe why the merger is happening and how the boards and trustees took detailed steps to make sure that the merger is fair to employees. Explain what will happen to their stock and what, if any, changes will occur in their ESOPs; what, if any, changes will occur to their benefits and compensation; the new management structure; and why you think this will help their ESOP account values grow.
- Set up an FAQ page on a website and seed it with key questions.
- Send out an explanation of the merger in plain English to their homes.
- Designate a team of nonmanagement people in each company to visit the other company and meet their new colleagues.

The merger or acquisition is a great opportunity to grow your ownership culture. Each company is likely to have its own strengths and weaknesses in getting employees involved in sharing information and generating new ideas. A joint culture committee of managers and nonmanagement employees should explore what is working in each company on such practices as open-book management, employee teams, suggestion systems, employee committees, and so on to develop a set of best practices to establish at each company.

Appendix: Survey Questions for Key Participants to Assess Mergers and Acquisitions

To construct this survey, a company needs to create a survey instrument with a five-point scale from strongly agree to agree to neutral to disagree to strongly disagree. The NCEO also has a detailed, customizable ownership culture survey specifically on employee ownership attitudes.[2]

Merger Assessment Questionnaire

1. I know exactly what is expected of me in my job in the new corporate structure.
2. The merger has made it easier for me to have the resources I need to get my job done.
3. The merger has made it harder for me to work with others.
4. In the new structure, my job makes at least as good use of my skills and abilities as was the case before the merger.
5. At work, my opinions seem to count at least as much as before the merger.
6. The people I work with generally believe the merger has been a good decision.
7. Because of the merger, I am more likely to look for a new job in the next year.
8. Because of the merger, at least some of my coworkers are more likely to look for a new job in the next year.
9. The mission and values of the merged companies are clear.
10. The merger has added new responsibilities that I do not feel comfortable with.
11. The merger has created conflicts with people in the other company.

---

2. See www.nceo.org/oc-survey.

12. I understand the process of change resulting from the merger.
13. We are making progress toward achieving the merger's goals.

Effects of Merger on the ESOP and Ownership Culture

1. The merger has made people:
   a. Feel less like owners
   b. Feel more like owners
   c. Has not affected ownership attitudes
2. The merger has made people believe the value of their ESOP is more likely to:
   a. Go up
   b. Stay the same
   c. Go down
3. The merger has made people:
   a. More secure about their job security
   b. Less secure about their job security
   c. Has not affected perceptions of job security
4. How well do people understand the consequences of the merger:
   a. Not very well
   b. Somewhat
   c. Reasonably well
   d. Very well

Comments

What changes can be made in the way the merged companies now operate that would improve your ability to do your job well?

CHAPTER 6

A Step-by-Step Guide to Pursuing Acquisitions

Corey Rosen

IT HAS BECOME EXTREMELY COMMON for ESOP companies to either make acquisitions or at least consider them. ESOP companies have several competitive advantages in the acquisition market. For many sellers, selling to an existing ESOP company means they can help preserve their company's legacy, ensure that the employees who helped build it are treated well, and get a fair price. In some cases, sellers may be able to defer taxation on the gain from the sale to an ESOP company. In a 2015 study,[1] Suzanne Cromlish, then at Case Western Reserve University, interviewed 30 ESOP company executives at companies that had performed an acquisition. The study showed that 442 of the 467 acquisitions were considered successful, compared with data indicating that 50%–80% of non-ESOP-related mergers fail to deliver positive results. This is largely due to the organizational values of ESOP companies, including open-book management, high-involvement planning, and careful integration of the acquired company. ESOP company acquisitions may also be less driven by the kind of CEO empire-building found in some non-ESOP company acquisitions.

1. Suzanne Cromlish, "Empowering the 99%...One ESOP at a Time! A Qualitative Study of Employee-Owned Company Acquisitions" (January 1, 2015), *Student Scholarship* 185, https://commons.case.edu/studentworks/185.

Companies need to decide on the acquisition structure. If the goal is diversification or acquiring different types of businesses, establishing a holding company could be an approach for having a basket of stocks all folded into one ESOP. Another reason could be acquiring a business with a brand and/or reputation you would like to maintain. As business activity ebbs and flows, having a variety of businesses or competencies can help to counter any downturn that happens in one of the businesses and smooth out the various business cycles. Holding companies create an opportunity for establishing shared services with a team within the holding company that maintains HR, IT, corporate strategy, and more. Companies in this structure can also maintain a degree of separation, with separate benefits, policies, and cultures. On the downside, it can be more difficult to create a cohesive culture and team camaraderie across multiple companies, or to find that glue that holds it all together. This can be especially true when people work in different industries, geographies, and branches. With a one-company approach, it is still possible to diversify and expand while integrating new businesses and employees into the existing company. From a cultural standpoint, the messaging of a single company, brand, and management team may influence the overall decision.

This discussion is necessarily simplistic, and it is worth noting that there is nuance to all of these factors. Neither structure is better than the other; the best structure is the one most appropriate for your company (which can change over time). There are many successful ESOP holding companies with wildly different businesses that all operate successfully under the holding company. At the same time, countless ESOP companies have successfully integrated acquired companies into their brands and cultures. Strategy should determine the best path forward.

Companies also need to consider whether it is worth structuring the transaction so that sellers of the target company can take the Section 1042 tax deferral on the gain from the sale to the ESOP company. While there are different approaches to doing this, the most common and the most reliable is for the target company to set up an ESOP financed by the acquirer. The target's ESOP buys out the owner, who can then reinvest in stocks and bonds of US operating companies and defer taxation on the gain until those securities are sold. Once the transaction is complete, the target company ESOP and the parent company ESOP merge. Because this involves the extra cost of setting up a second ESOP, it is practical only in larger transactions where the purchase price can be reduced to reflect some or all of the value to the seller.

Acquisitions are time-consuming, often complicated, and sometimes risky. Companies need to develop a thorough process for both identifying potential targets and integrating the acquired company into the parent company. Depending on the structure, there may be additional legal complexities and costs. Below is a detailed roadmap for approaching acquisitions. It describes how companies can think about the acquisition opportunity and process. Some of the items appear under more than one section because they are relevant in more than one area. The list was developed with input from multiple ESOP company executives and advisors: Mike Hart from EEEA Consulting Engineers; Chris Fredericks from Empowered Ventures; Doug Bawel from Jasper Holdings; Michael Quarrey from Web Industries; Daniel Goldstein, formerly with Folience; and Mary Josephs from Verit Advisors. We at the NCEO greatly appreciate their assistance.

The NCEO maintains a directory of acquisitive ESOP companies.[2] If your company is considering doing acquisitions, you may want to add your name to the directory. The directory is useful both for companies seeking to sell to an ESOP company and for business brokers. We also have a toolkit[3] for companies seeking to be acquired by an ESOP.

A Roadmap for Approaching Acquisitions

Should We Do It?

1. Do we need to do acquisitions to maintain our position in the marketplace?
2. Does the business have a clear organic growth strategy that works and is producing excess cash flow beyond what the organic strategy requires to support?

---

2. See https://www.nceo.org/acquisitive-esop-directory.
3. See https://www.nceo.org/resource-toolkits/being-acquired-esop-company-toolkit.

3. Has the company come close to exhausting organic growth opportunities, which can often be less risky and less expensive?
4. What happens if we do not pursue acquisitions? Can we grow sufficiently on our own?
5. Will staff diverted to acquisitions be better used on other projects?
6. Do we need to borrow money, and is the debt affordable?
7. Is it important to diversify? What are the risks of diversifying?
8. Do we have a team eager to tackle additional growth and challenges beyond what is right in front of us?
9. Do we have the ability to bifurcate our operation, with a core team focused on our business and a separate team focused on acquisitions?
10. Are there attractive options in the market, or are most potential targets overpriced?
11. Should we consider buying distressed firms either for their potential or just for their talent?
12. Do we have a supportive board and trustee?

Purpose of M&A

1. Accelerate growth of shareholder value by acquiring companies that provide vertical, horizontal, or adjacent industry firms.
2. Grow equity value by increasing total EBITDA, reducing risk, reducing the discount rate in the valuation, targeting at least x% over current revenue or EBITDA, or increasing the multiple.
3. Put surplus capital to work for greater returns by creating a greater margin of safety. Surplus capital is capital that is more than that needed for emergencies, cyclical expenses, and repurchase obligations.
4. Create synergies with acquisitions into new markets for organic growth. This can include introducing current products and services into new markets, introducing new products and services

into existing markets, and entering new markets whose risk counterbalances risks in the company (cyclicality, client concentration, etc.).

5. Allow growth opportunities for current employees to move into management positions.
6. Diversify holdings to reduce risk.
7. Strengthen cash flow to meet future repurchase obligations without overreliance on debt or dilution.
8. Access strategic capabilities; acquire specialized skills, technology, equipment, certifications, or customer relationships that would be costly or slow to develop organically.
9. Create new opportunities if our organic growth opportunities are limited or exhausted.

Due Diligence Topic Areas

1. Legal
2. Accounting and tax
3. Human resources
4. Health insurance and benefits
5. Safety
6. Commercial insurance
7. Information technology
8. Market/competitor analysis
9. Real estate/environmental
10. Customers and vendors

How Often Should We Pursue an Acquisition?

1. Only when an opportunity presents itself, or do we seek out acquisitions?

2. What financial reserve needs do we have for other purposes (cyclicality, emergencies, repurchase, etc.) before we can pursue an acquisition?
3. Only if we have sufficient staff capacity to do acquisitions?

Geographic Growth

1. Identify common traits of attractive new geographic markets:
    - Presence of existing clients who are growing.
    - Presence of strengths and prospects in an industry where we have strengths and growth prospects.
    - Low volume and quality of competitor firms.
    - Desirable location (so employee-owners may want to relocate).
    - Presence of higher education or other resources for potential new hires.
    - Consider the additional reporting (taxes, etc.) required when entering a new state.
2. Will in-person travel between companies happen, and if so, how regularly?
3. Consider whether geographic differences across industries, cultural differences, etc., will derail M&A success if not anticipated and navigated effectively.

Target Characteristics

1. High engagement culture, employee-centered
2. Loyal client base
3. Next generation of leadership identified
4. Possible competitive advantages
5. Companies with an aging owner and strong second-level leaders who do not have the funds to buy out the owner
6. Companies in market sectors we value with turnaround potential

7. Opportunities for broad cross-selling of our new capabilities to the company's current core capabilities. Expanding the company's market share with existing clients; up-tiering relationships with existing clients; better conversions on new client acquisition (this often includes adjacent products and services).

How We Do It

1. Create a budget and timeline:
    - Sources of cash
    - Specify an individual or team to spend time internally
    - Hire an outside M&A firm?
2. Identify targets. Create an initial screening checklist to help filter down the initial list; what criteria can we evaluate based on internet data and a teaser document or confidential information memorandum?
3. Heatmap SWOT: identify which specific capabilities best complement our strengths and weaknesses.

Screen Targets and Complete the Transaction

1. Meet with key seller stakeholders.
2. Meet with leaders and assess culture.
3. Define what benefits accrue to the company.
4. Complete a go/no-go evaluation.
5. Offer a letter of intent.
6. Know what not to share as the evaluation progresses. Guard the most secret information until closer to a deal (definitely do not share key personal information). Have nonsolicitation agreements with key personnel. Never show client lists.
7. Share data and interview relevant parties.
8. Prove up data and forecasts.

9. Negotiate a purchase or merger contract.
10. Complete and execute the contract.
11. Fit with leadership culture.
12. Potential legal issues.
13. Target liability issues.
14. Will others bid on the same company and drive up the price?
15. Securing experienced M&A counsel is recommended. Know who is representing the seller and have counsel of a similar caliber.
16. Negotiate the purchase or merger contract:
    - Understand the myriad of negotiation details relating to the stock purchase agreement (SPA).
    - Understand who holds what liabilities (buyer versus seller).
    - Understand seller indemnifications and holdbacks.

Financing

1. What kind of structure is our bank (or another senior lender) willing to provide to support acquisitions, and is that sufficient for the opportunities we expect to see and the desired pace we want to have?
2. If not, is higher-cost debt practical, or would it be better to bring in an equity partner?
3. What is our risk tolerance for debt?
4. Does our team or valuation firm have the ability to continually assess how we understand the value and the valuation of diversification?
5. Can the target bring added debt capacity?

Define the Integration Process

1. Designate the integration team at our company and at the target. Do we prefer to build an in-house capability for finding and culti-

vating opportunities? Or would we prefer to engage an intermediary who will find opportunities on our behalf?

2. Who is on our deal team? Do they have sufficient M&A experience?
3. Do we need to supplement our current team to have the bandwidth to complete acquisitions?
4. Do we need to consider our board's composition? What is the role of the board? What is the role of the trustee? What are business decisions versus fiduciary decisions?
5. Develop a transition plan for the integration path.
6. Decide on systems, pay, benefits, and other administrative integration issues.
7. Build/integrate a company culture to become one firm.
8. Define expected outcomes during the process, measure and adjust as needed, and track and communicate progress.

Appendix: Further Resources

Directory

NCEO Directory of Acquisitive ESOP Companies (https://www.nceo.org/acquisitive-esop-directory)

Toolkit

NCEO Being Acquired by an ESOP Company Toolkit (https://www.nceo.org/resource-toolkits/being-acquired-esop-company-toolkit)

Events

The NCEO Annual Conference (https://annualconference.nceo.org/) features ample content on acquisition basics, strategy, integration, and more.

The NCEO Forum (https://forum.nceo.org/) also offers broad coverage of acquisitions.

CHAPTER 7

M&A Strategy: The Essential Steps to Growing ESOP Companies Through Acquisitions

Mary Josephs and Dustin Kim

The ESOP Advantage in Acquisitions

It has become increasingly common for ESOP companies to pursue acquisitions, and for good reason. ESOP companies possess competitive advantages that their non-ESOP peers cannot easily replicate. For owners looking to sell their business, selling to an existing ESOP company means preserving the legacy of their business, ensuring employees who helped build it are treated well, and receiving a fair price. A 2015 study by Suzanne Cromlish at Case Western Reserve University found that 442 of 467 ESOP company acquisitions were considered successful, a remarkable result compared to the widely cited data showing 50%–80% of non-ESOP mergers fail to deliver positive results. The researchers attributed ESOP success to organizational values, including open-book management, high-involvement planning, and careful integration. ESOP acquisitions may also be less prone to the empire-building tendencies that undermine value in some non-ESOP transactions.

When you are in front of a prospective seller,[1] lean into this story. Employee ownership, long-term culture preservation, and legacy continuity are genuine differentiators that resonate with owners who have spent decades building something meaningful. Learn to tell that story early and tell it well.

Why Create an M&A Strategy?

Before pursuing growth through M&A, firms must recognize that M&A is an extension of their broader corporate strategy, not a strategy in itself. Leadership must first clearly define the firm's long-term direction.

An M&A strategy is best understood as a subset of a company's overall growth strategy, which may also include organic growth, new products, new markets, and talent acquisition to deepen capabilities. When considering whether M&A is the right lever, it helps to anchor the rationale in one of three value drivers: scale (cost savings and efficiency), scope (entering new markets), or capabilities (acquiring new skills and technology).

In creating an M&A strategy, the first step should always be an assessment of the company's strategic plan, including its growth tactics. M&A can be more expensive than organic growth in both dollars and management bandwidth, and one of the most costly resources is management and leadership time. Many ESOP companies seek out potential targets themselves, often drawing on their industry knowledge. All too often, however, companies without a defined acquisition strategy become "reactive" to promotional materials from investment bankers trying to entice them to bid on the company the bankers are getting paid to sell. This can be a sinkhole distracting your attention from higher-priority initiatives. Remember that those seeking to persuade you to buy a business are highly motivated to get you interested.

A clear and thoughtful strategy helps clarify what leadership should focus on. To begin, perform a thoughtful review, often through a SWOT (strengths, weaknesses, opportunities, and threats) analysis.

1. In many cases, the first audience is not the seller but the seller's service providers.

This can be done internally or with an independent consultant to work with leadership to assess and design an M&A strategy. A well-defined M&A strategy will tell you:

- Is M&A an appropriate part of your growth strategy? Are you better off pursuing organic growth opportunities? Or perhaps cleaning up operational gaps to improve efficiency and margins?
- What company size should you be looking at? Simply narrowing the "what" you choose to look at based on your company's risk tolerance and debt capacity will be a time-saver.
- What niche should you be looking for? This is based on assessing your current geographical footprint, products and services, risks and opportunities, opportunities for diversification, and under-leveraged or overtaxed capabilities.
- Does your management team have the capacity to execute an acquisition?

Conduct a Self-Assessment

Before committing to an acquisition strategy, leadership should work through the following questions. These are drawn from the collective experience of ESOP executives and advisors who have led successful acquisitions as well as those who have learned the hard way when critical questions are overlooked.

- Does the business have a clear organic growth strategy that is working and producing excess cash flow beyond what the organic strategy requires?
- Has the company come close to exhausting organic growth opportunities, which are often less risky and less expensive than acquisitions?
- Do we need to borrow money to pursue acquisitions, and is the debt load affordable given our repurchase obligations, capital requirements, and liquidity needs?

- Do we have a supportive board and trustee who understand and are aligned with an acquisition strategy?
- Does our management team have the experience to evaluate, operate, and grow an acquired business?

Developing Your Acquisition Strategy

With the "why" and the "self-assessment" established, the next step is developing the acquisition strategy. The answer starts with translating your corporate vision into a concrete, actionable framework and then making deliberate choices about where to grow, how to grow, and what kind of target will get you there.

1. Identify Your Growth Path: Build, Borrow, or Buy

Before committing to acquisitions, companies should rigorously evaluate three paths to growth: "build, borrow, or buy." Building organically through internal investment, product development, and market penetration is often the least expensive and most controllable path. Borrowing through alliances, joint ventures, and licensing arrangements can accelerate growth without the full commitment and risk of acquisition. Buying through M&A is the fastest path to scale but carries the highest execution risk. According to Bain research, 75% of growth initiatives fail, and related acquisitions fail at a 70% rate. Acquisitions should therefore be reserved for situations where building or borrowing would clearly fall short in terms of speed, uniqueness of assets, or competitive necessity.

Think of how companies have applied this framework in practice. An industrial services firm might build new service lines organically by training existing crews, borrow capabilities through a subcontracting arrangement with a specialty firm, or buy a regional competitor outright to enter a new geographic region quickly. The right answer depends on time horizon, balance sheet capacity, and how critical the capability is to the core. What matters most is that the choice is deliberate, not default. Many companies fall into acquisitions reactively simply because a deal appeared, rather than because it was the best path to their strategic objective.

2. Avoid the Temptation to Stray from Core

Knowing which of the three rationales drives your deal is important, but equally important is not letting that rationale stretch too far. Scope claims deserve particular scrutiny. History is littered with examples of companies that stretched the logic of adjacency too far. More recently, WeWork's attempt to reframe real estate leasing as a technology and community business ultimately collapsed. Peloton aggressively expanded into apparel and accessories during the COVID-19 pandemic, distracting from its core connected fitness offering at the wrong moment. Many regional service businesses have stumbled by acquiring companies in adjacent industries where they lacked the operational expertise, vendor relationships, or customer knowledge that made them successful at home. For ESOP companies in particular, an overreaching acquisition can jeopardize not just financial returns but the culture and employee ownership model that took years to build. The further a deal strays from the core, the weaker the competitive advantage and the lower the probability of success.

3. Use the Ansoff Matrix and Adjacency Framework to Define Growth Areas

Two frameworks are worth keeping close when you start evaluating where to grow. The first is the Ansoff Growth Matrix,[2] which maps growth across two axes: existing versus new products, and existing versus new markets. The four resulting paths are market penetration, product expansion, market expansion, and diversification. The further right and down you move on that matrix, the harder the deal gets. (See figure 7-1.)

The second is the Bain/Zook adjacency model, which is just a way of asking how many steps this is from what you already do well. One or two steps out, say a new geography or a complementary service line, and you can usually lean on existing customer relationships, vendor networks, and operational know-how. Three or four steps out, and

2. Adapted from H. Igor Ansoff, "Strategies for Diversification," *Harvard Business Review*, September-October 1957.

MARKETS	EXISTING PRODUCTS	NEW PRODUCTS
	Market penetration Sell more to existing customers and grow share of wallet in markets you already serve. *ESOP example: Add crews or capacity in geographies where you already operate.* **Lowest risk**	**Product expansion** Introduce new services to your existing customer base. *ESOP example: HVAC company adds plumbing or electrical services.* **Moderate risk**
	Market expansion Take your existing services into new geographies or customer segments. *ESOP example: Regional distributor acquires a competitor in an adjacent territory.* **Moderate risk**	**Diversification** Enter new markets with new products—the highest-complexity growth move. *ESOP example: Manufacturing firm acquires an unrelated software company.* **Highest risk**

Risk increases →

Figure 7-1. Ansoff growth matrix

you're essentially starting over in a business you don't understand yet. Amazon is the textbook example of getting this right: books to e-commerce, e-commerce to AWS (built on infrastructure they already ran), AWS to logistics. Each move extended something they already had.

For ESOP companies, this matters more than most people realize. A facilities management company buying a janitorial firm is one step out. Buying a security technology company is three or four: different customers, different hiring profile, different vendor relationships entirely. That's not growth, that's a bet. And ESOP companies don't have the luxury of unlimited bets. Management time, borrowing capacity, and the confidence of a workforce that has real skin in the game are all finite. Stretch too far, and you don't just risk the return, you risk the culture and the ownership model that took years to build.

4. Establish Screening Criteria

Once the strategic rationale and growth areas are defined, the next step is building a screening rubric to evaluate potential acquisitions consistently. Without one, the process becomes subjective and time-

Criteria	Weight	Target 1	Target 2
Portfolio, IP, differentiation	25%	Differentiated IP Weighted: 1.25	Offer that will fit portfolio Weighted: 0.75
Segments, clients	20%	Focus on market segment not profitable Weighted: 0.80	Focus on market segment that is profitable Weighted: 0.40
Revenue, margin/EBITDA	20%	Profitability Weighted: 0.40	Profit margins Weighted: 0.60
Delivery, business development	20%	Business development Weighted: 0.40	Team capability Weighted: 0.20
Operating model, culture	15%	Fit for differentiated practices Weighted: 0.45	Molding practices into advisory practices Weighted: 0.75
Weighted total score Weights sum to 100%	100%	**3.30** Recommended	**2.70**

Figure 7-2. Sample screening criteria rubric

consuming. Figure 7-2 shows how a simple weighted scorecard works: assign each criterion a weight that reflects its importance to your strategy, score each target from 1 to 5, and identify targets with the highest weighted average score.

For ESOP companies, culture and organizational alignment deserve more weight than a non-ESOP buyer would assign. Your employees are owners, and a poorly integrated acquisition can disrupt the culture that made your company worth acquiring in the first place.

5. Find Your Targets

Once the strategy and screening criteria are in place, the work shifts to identifying targets. Start with a large universe. The final list will be short, but casting too narrow a net risks missing companies that would have made the cut. With the parameters set, here are four ways to build that universe. Finding targets is more art than science, as this section will touch on.

Go Get It Yourself

The most effective acquirers don't wait for the phone to ring. They build deliberate relationships long before a target is ready to sell. Think of it like dating: if you know exactly what you are looking for, you'll recognize it when you see it, and the right introduction is rarely more than a degree or two away.

The first place to look is right in front of you. Your leadership team, sales staff, customers, and suppliers have built relationships in your space over the years. Involve your organization in building a first list of potential targets. They are the ones with ears to the ground and may know more than you expect.

Show up where your targets show up. Attend trade associations, industry conferences, roundtables, and community events. Talk to your accountants, attorneys, consultants, bankers, and brokers. Tell them what you are looking for.

Managing and maintaining the pipeline is where most companies fall short. A watch list is not a spreadsheet you update twice a year. Like a plant, it needs constant care to bear fruit. Keeping the pipeline warm is an active discipline, not a passive one. An effective pipeline looks like this:

- Monitor targets continuously and reprioritize as businesses evolve and new names emerge.
- Tier your targets as not every prospect deserves the same attention, and your time is your scarcest resource.
- Nurture relationships with top targets over months and years, not days. People sell to people they trust.
- Find ways to collaborate before any deal is on the table. Copresent at a conference, host a lunch-and-learn, or simply make an introduction.

Be intentional about it. Once rapport is established, the most important thing you can communicate is why joining your company would be good for them and their people. If you're already an ESOP company, the story of employee ownership and culture preservation is a genuine differentiator that you should learn to tell early.

The best deals are proprietary. A seller who calls you before going to market will almost always result in better pricing and terms than a competitive process. This kind of sourcing takes years to build, sometimes decades. But once the flywheel starts turning, it is hard to slow down.

Be Selectively Reactive

Deals will come to you unsolicited, from investment bankers running sell-side processes, business brokers, and owners who heard through the grapevine that you are in the market to buy. You will be able to discard many of these quickly at first glance.

The key here is speed and clarity. With a well-defined acquisition profile, you can quickly assess whether an inbound opportunity fits your criteria. You need to build the mental muscle to quickly discard the ones that don't fit. As we keep repeating, your management team's time is the scarcest resource, and even more so during an M&A process. A poorly fitting deal will consume time, energy, and attention that could be better spent elsewhere.

One important dynamic to understand is that when an investment banker presents you with a target, you should assume that you are entering a competitive process. The seller has hired an advisor to maximize the business's value and create tension among potential buyers. That is the job of the investment banker. This is not to say you should pass on every banker-led deal, but apply heightened scrutiny to those opportunities, as you are likely to pay a premium versus a proprietary deal.

Hire a Buy-Side Advisor

If the steps above seem impractical given your bandwidth, or your timeline is too compressed to build meaningful relationships, you can hire a buy-side advisor, a professional paid on retainer to identify and present acquisition targets on your behalf.

When it works, it works well. There are excellent buy-side advisors who bring deep networks, rigorous screening, and real market intelligence. Quality varies considerably, however, and the incentive structure deserves scrutiny. Buy-side advisors are typically paid a monthly retainer plus a success fee at closing. That means there is some incentive to show you deal flow, even if it doesn't match your criteria, to justify the retainer and remain positioned for a success fee.

Before engaging a buy-side advisor, ask the hard questions:

- What is your experience as an advisor, and how successful have you been?
- Can you provide references from past clients, including unsuccessful deals?

Consider creating certain milestones when you do engage with a buy-side advisor, and don't be afraid to terminate the relationship if they are not producing as expected early in the process. A good buy-side advisor should be able to know within a few weeks if the search is viable by talking to their network. Companies that skip these guardrails sometimes find themselves with months of work and thousands (sometimes hundreds of thousands) of dollars down the drain with nothing to show for it.

Build an Internal Corporate Development Team

Companies serious about growing through acquisitions should consider building a dedicated corporate development team that functions as an internal buy-side advisor. While an external buy-side advisor can be valuable, they often lack a deep understanding of your company's culture, strategic priorities, and long-term objectives.

An internal corporate development team can build and maintain industry relationships, develop proprietary sourcing channels, and keep a consistent pipeline of high-quality acquisition targets aligned with your company's interests. If acquisitions are expected to be a meaningful driver of long-term growth, standing up a corporate development team may be worth considering. This doesn't have to be a large team. For many ESOP companies, it can start with a single dedicated hire and build from there on out.

Choosing Your Approach

If you're unsure which approach to use to find acquisition targets, start with the first approach above: go get it yourself. Begin by getting the word out in your industry and building relationships organically. Embed this mindset across your management team and broader employee base so deal sourcing becomes a natural extension of how the firm operates.

As you gain traction and comfort, begin expanding your reach by reviewing opportunities brought in by investment bankers and testing whether engaging a buy-side advisor adds value to your sourcing strategy. After you go through one or two acquisitions, you'll be in a position to identify internal talent that has shown the aptitude and fortitude to lead the corporate development team.

How to Execute the Strategy

Once the acquisition strategy is in place and a target has been identified, the work shifts to executing and closing the transaction. Even with a well-defined strategy and aligned goals, a deal will demand significant time and resources from your organization. The cost is real and should not be underestimated. However, for ESOP companies that stay disciplined through the process, the result is a stronger, more diversified business that compounds value for every employee-owner. The three phases below are the steps to executing and closing the transaction.

Phase One: Qualify and Pursue

Finding a target that fits your criteria is only the beginning. Before going further, ask again what exactly the target does for your company. Much of that thought process occurred during screening, but it deserves a fresh look. A target company that looks attractive on paper can lose its appeal once you start digging under the hood. The goal in this phase is to make a go/no-go decision.

Consider what the deal-breakers are that would make you lose sleep at night. Is there a valuation gap? Does the team culture align with yours? Is there a customer concentration risk that would hinder the business going forward? Whatever it is, write them down.

As an ESOP company, make sure your balance sheet can carry the deal. If you are still paying down debt from your own ESOP transaction, the new acquisition would strain your balance sheet and ability to fund repurchase obligations. You also need to take the ESOP trustee into consideration. Although the trustee does not approve the deal, it will impact the share price, and a trustee that learns of it later in the process will not appreciate last-minute surprises. Keep the trustee informed early on if possible.

Another important part of this phase of the process is to meet the target's management team in person, ideally at their headquarters. This allows you to walk down the hallways, get a feel of the company's culture, and have the opportunity to tell your story. Explain how becoming an ESOP has benefited your company, but most importantly, the upside it has provided for your employees who are now owners. Stories like this will resonate and can set you apart from other potential buyers at the table, especially with a target who cares about legacy.

Once there is mutual interest, and before any meaningful information changes hands, both sides sign a non-disclosure agreement (NDA). With the NDA in place, the next step is to submit a letter of intent (LOI) to the target. The LOI is a non-binding letter expressing your preliminary interest in acquiring the target. It typically covers a description of your business, the purpose of the acquisition, the purchase price, what due diligence items you expect to cover, a period of exclusivity, and your intentions for the target's management team, among others.

Phase Two: Diligence

Once the target has accepted the LOI, the most demanding phase of the transaction begins, due diligence. Due diligence will drain management's time and attention, and this is where deal fatigue sets in and tests the patience of both sides. Due diligence entails setting up a secure data room, a quality-of-earnings review of the target's financials, analysis of key customers and contracts, a legal and tax review, and a hard and honest look at the people that you are counting on to stay on as new employee-owners. The workload is higher than most acquirers expect, so do not underestimate the burden it places on your team. If your company has not been through an acquisition before, hiring an investment banker is recommended. They quarterback the workstreams, manage the request list, and keep the target responsive, keeping the chaos of the transaction organized and on schedule.

It is important to set clear expectations with the respective managers who will lead each workstream from accounting and tax, legal, human resources, benefits, information technology, and operations, to name a few. At smaller companies, which many ESOP sponsors are, much of this burden may fall on one or two individuals, so plan around their capacity and bring in outside advisors where the internal bench is thin.

Diligence is the opportunity to ask the tough questions and leave no stone unturned. If something surfaces that gives you a pause, take that pause. Decide whether it is a real problem or an issue that can be addressed or priced into the deal. If it cannot, draw a line in the sand and walk away, even if significant time and money have already been spent. Sunk costs are a bad reason to buy the wrong company. Deals are won and lost on diligence, but companies are lost when management takes its eye off the business.

Phase Three: Negotiate and Close

Once due diligence is complete and you have a better understanding of and comfort with the target, it is time to move on to the final phase. Ideally, you will have already engaged an experienced M&A counsel by this point. Hiring counsel early is highly recommended, as the legal workstream is demanding and poorly drafted agreements can derail a deal or worse, close on terms and conditions that will haunt you later.

During negotiation, lean on your advisors[3] to drive the terms and negotiations, such as valuation, net working capital peg, treatment

3. The advisors include investment bankers, legal counsel, tax advisors, and accountants. For ESOP companies, the trustee and the trustee's independent counsel and valuation advisor are also part of the picture.

of debt and debt-like items, representations and warranties, and any indemnification holdbacks that affect the net purchase price. The banker's job is to keep the negotiation grounded in what diligence uncovered. If the quality-of-earnings work revealed customer concentration, questionable margins, or people problems, those findings should make their way into the purchase price, the deal structure, or contractual protections. Sometimes they should make you walk away entirely. The banker and counsel should be working side by side, with the banker handling the economics and counsel handling the legal portions respectively, keeping you and the board informed.

The negotiated terms all land in the definitive documents, anchored by the purchase agreement, which ultimately governs the transaction, so getting it right is critical. The purchase agreement doesn't travel alone. Disclosure schedules qualify the seller's representations and should be read as carefully as the agreement itself, including ancillary documents such as escrow agreements, employment agreements, and any transition service arrangements. As you can see, there is a hefty amount of legal work that needs to be completed, so hiring a good attorney is critical to help navigate through the choppy waters. This is when the sellers and their counsel push the hardest, and where, if you are inexperienced, you can give away value without even realizing it.

For ESOP owners, there is an additional layer to consider: the trustee. By this point in the process, the trustee should already be aware of the transaction and have a good understanding of what the deal entails, as the acquisition ultimately needs to be evaluated against whether it serves the long-term interests of employee-owners. A well-documented process is as critical as the negotiation itself.

With the definitive documents negotiated and closing conditions satisfied, it is time to sign and close the deal. Take a moment and take a breather to recognize the hard work you and your team have done to get to this point. However, the work doesn't stop here, as consideration must be given to employee communication, integration, and post-transaction work.

Integration: The Key Often-Missed Step

Closing a deal is not the finish line; it is the starting gun. The acquisitions that deliver lasting value are those in which integration is treated with the same discipline and preparation as the transaction itself. For ESOP companies, the stakes are higher since you are not just combining operations; you are extending an ownership culture to a new group of employees. How you handle the first 90 days will shape whether those employees become genuine owners in mindset, or simply new hires who happen to work for an ESOP company.

To aid in the integration, it is helpful to put an integration team in place. The integration team, which should include the general counsel, CFO, and heads of your organization's respective departments, should be engaged during diligence, not after. They need to understand what they are inheriting, build relationships with their counterparts at the target, and identify the pressure points before day one. Waiting until closing to assemble this team is one of the most common and costly integration mistakes.

Create a well-detailed integration roadmap with clear swim lanes for each department to keep people accountable and on track. A simple project tracker with owners and deadlines will do more for a clean integration than any amount of goodwill. Assign a single integration manager who owns the overall timeline and reports directly to the CEO and the board.

This is a nervous time for your existing employees, especially the newly acquired ones. For that reason, communicate early, often, and with intention. Silence is the enemy of integration. Employees at the acquired company will fill any information vacuum with anxiety and rumors. Before day one, leadership should have a clear message prepared: who you are, why this combination makes sense, what will change, what will not change, and what the path to ESOP participation looks like.

Finally, measure integration progress the same way you measure business performance, with metrics and accountability. Track milestones against the plan, surface problems early, and do not declare victory prematurely. The best acquirers conduct a formal integration review at 90 days and again at one year, asking honestly what worked, what did not, and what they would do differently next time. That discipline, applied repeatedly, is what separates companies that grow well through acquisitions from those that simply grow.

Conclusion

Don't start an M&A process by randomly chasing targets or sporadically responding to inbound solicitations from bankers enticing you to buy a company they are selling. Take a pause. Develop the "why and how" that will drive shareholder value. When M&A presents compelling opportunities in accord with your strategy, qualify them rigorously, diligence them thoroughly, and integrate with intention.

The acquisition process can be long, and at times it can feel like there is no end in sight. Deal fatigue is real, and it tests both sides. During those stretches, remember why you decided to pursue the target in the first place. Keep the acquisition strategy aligned with the corporate strategy, not the other way around. Build genuine relationships with other stakeholders early on, instill an acquisition mindset across your organization, and seek help when needed. Know that as an ESOP company, you carry an advantage no other buyer can match: legacy and culture. Sellers care about what happens to their company and their people after the wire hits, and no buyer tells the story better than one owned by its employees. Tell the story early, tell it often, and let it be the reason the next great company chooses to join your family of employee-owners.

CHAPTER 8

ESOP Company Acquisition Case Studies

Mary Josephs, Dustin Kim, Corey Rosen, and Carter Wideman

THIS CHAPTER presents case studies of seven businesses in a range of sizes that offer different perspectives on how acquisitions can help ESOP-owned companies thrive: Border States, HB Global, Hypertherm, Jasper Holdings, Proponent, Empowered Ventures, and Roush Auto Group.

Border States

Acquiring Scale and Talent Through Acquisitions and Infusing an Employee-Owned Culture

Mary Josephs and Dustin Kim

Border States is a supply chain solutions company focused on distributing electrical, natural gas, PVF, MRO, and other products to its customers. Border States implemented an ESOP in 1984 and has since grown from $40 million in sales to more than $5 billion through many acquisitions and geographic expansion to 32 states and counting. Two factors have contributed to Border States' success: industry-wide consolidation that rewards scale, and an internal philosophy that sees acquisitions not only as a tool for geographic, industry, and customer expansion but also as a vehicle for acquiring talent aligned with Border States' culture and values to support continued growth and leadership development.

Industry consolidation has been the backdrop for Border States' growth since it began its acquisition path at the turn of the century. Customers and manufacturers both pushed distributors toward consolidation: customers expect their distributors to follow them into new geographies, and manufacturers increasingly prefer to concentrate their business with fewer, more meaningful partnerships based on size and the ability to grow the success of both parties, versus maintaining hundreds of smaller ones that require more time, energy, and resources to grow. For Border States, acquisitions have been the mechanism for managing both risks and opportunities created by this industry consolidation over the years. The risk is managed by becoming a larger, more diversified company in a consolidating industry, and the opportunities come through a combined platform that consistently outperforms what either company could achieve on a stand-alone basis. One acquired company in the Carolinas, for example, had relationships and a trusted partnership with a customer, but had previously been unable to pursue large-scale projects with that customer due to financial constraints. However, within months of joining Border States, the new employee-owners were positioned to handle a nearly $50 million opportunity, showcasing the strength of combining local service and relationships with the scale and resources of a larger organization.

While Border States' acquisition rationale began with geography and customer needs, talent and culture have become the dominant lens through which it now evaluates targets. For example, one-third of its current executive team members are employee-owners who joined Border States through acquisitions. Border States continually seeks new talent in its acquisitions and works to place the new employees in the roles that best suit them, aligning the acquired employee-owners' desires and skills with the needs of the larger organization.

As Border States has grown organically and through acquisitions, now at 3,800-plus employee-owners, sustaining a strong, positive culture of employee ownership through its pace of acquisition has required intentional effort. Border States has an employee-owner credo and maintains a set of "ownership essentials" that it expects all of its employee-owners to follow to deliver their best work. Managers are encouraged to tie everyday efforts explicitly back to the ownership essentials, reinforcing them through consistent feedback, recognition, and storytelling. The storytelling has emerged as a particularly important pillar. Hearing how colleagues live out the Border States credo or ownership essentials helps new employee-owners, especially those who joined through acquisitions, see themselves immersed in the company's employee ownership culture. These three pillars are how Border States maintains its culture even as it acquires new companies and adds employee-owners while growing rapidly.

Border States relies on building long-term relationships to source deals rather than relying solely on brokers to identify potential acquisition opportunities. Most of Border States' acquisitions have originated through cultivating relationships with target company owners and executives over the years. Border States has a dedicated director of M&A who serves as a conduit to relationship building and operational excellence in executing the transaction and subsequent integration. Over its history of acquisitions, Border States has learned that unsuccessful deals have almost always been due to cultural misalignment. A target that has a deep care for its employees' futures and its own legacy often aligns well with Border States' acquisition success.

Over the years, Border States has enjoyed some great successes and experienced some failures with its acquisitions. For example, in one of Border States' earlier acquisitions, the target company's decisions were made by the owner, and Border States did not ask enough questions regarding the decision-making process. As a result, it became evident that employees lacked experience in decision-making and had not been given the authority to make decisions. As a result, some locations experienced a range of outcomes, from slow decision-making to no decision-making, while others found new motivation with the increased responsibility to make more decisions. As a result of this experience, a key part of Border States' diligence process became asking how the entity makes decisions and operates, to understand the level of autonomy people have to do their jobs.

One theme continues to emerge for Border States. When you give people a great environment to do their best work and an opportunity to share in the rewards of their hard work, they will thrive, to the benefit of their customers, their manufacturing partners, and for each other.

HB Global

Corey Rosen

According to HB Global's website:[1]

> HB Global, LLC is the parent company of 11 U.S. divisions in the mechanical, infrastructure, and real estate service industries. HB Global is based in Camp Hill, PA, and is proudly employee owned. The Company now has approximately 1,900 employee owners. Its divisions include HB McClure Company based in Harrisburg, PA, IT Landes Company based in Harleysville, PA, Nash Plumbing & Mechanical based in Belleview, FL, North Shore Mechanical Contractors based in Wilmington, MA, William R. Nash based in Tamarac, FL, The Bell Company based in Rochester, NY, BBEC based in Mechanicsburg, PA, DB Mechanical based in Salt Lake City, UT, Hyper Networks based in Pineville, NC, HB Home Services based in Harrisburg, PA, and Rhodes Development Group Companies based in Camp Hill, PA.
>
> HB Global is committed to acquisitions as part of its strategy for growth. Since 2011, we have completed over 30 successful acquisitions. Every acquisition is uniquely structured to fulfill their previous owners' retirement goals. We offer a collaborative process that allows flexibility for how your business fits into our organizational structure, which makes us a compelling and viable alternative to private equity for your succession planning needs.

In its acquisition book on its website,[2] the company notes that it is an alternative to private equity, something many sellers find appealing given private equity's mixed track record when it comes to preserving jobs. In contrast, 95% of employees at HB Global acquisitions stayed on after the purchase. The acquisition book quotes Bradford Osborne, former owner and current president of North Shore Mechanical, as

1. "Looking to Sell?," HB Global, accessed July 16, 2026, https://hb-global.com/acquisitions/.
2. "Creating Success Together: Continuing Your Legacy Through Employee Ownership," HB Global, embedded at https://hb-global.com/acquisitions/.

saying, "After putting 30 years into building North Shore Mechanical, I was looking for a long-term solution to transition out of having a partnership and still be very involved in the business I built. I was looking for a third party that was employee-focused and who could not only sustain the company but grow the business. HB Global's mission, core values, and ESOP was the complete package, and it has been instrumental in our success of our employees and our growth. HB Global's leadership's passion for what they were doing was clear from the first meeting throughout the process and proves true today."[3]

In a 2021 podcast,[4] HB Global's CEO Bob Whalen said that when seeking companies to acquire, HB Global looks for cultural alignment, e.g., a company that seeks to be a great place to work for employees and does great work for clients. While culture always comes first, the company looks for companies in markets that they are not currently serving or that are in adjacent industries. A major part of the strategy focuses on who will operate the business because HB Global gives acquired companies a lot of autonomy. Keeping current management is a priority, although some smaller "bolt-on" acquisitions are more integrated into HB Global and have less autonomy.

HB Global has a development team scouring potential targets, and they find one at least every week that is a general fit. But most only receive an initial review. The next stage is when they have a conversation. Of companies they talk to, perhaps 1 out of 15 to 20 becomes acquired.

Acquisitions allow HB Global to grow much faster, which is in line with the company's mission to expand employee ownership, something they believe is critical for society and communities. Acquisitions also create many opportunities for existing HB Global employees because the company is growing.

---

3. HB Global, "Creating Success Together: Continuing Your Legacy Through Employee Ownership," p. 5.
4. HB Global, "Acquisitions: What Makes a Good Fit?" (audio podcast), December 29, 2021, https://hb-capital.net/acquisitions-what-makes-a-good-fit/.

Hypertherm

Global Product Adjacency Expansion, One Culture

Mary Josephs and Carter Wideman

Hypertherm is a Hanover, New Hampshire-based manufacturer of industrial cutting products and related software, providing industry-leading plasma, laser, and waterjet solutions to customers worldwide. It became partially ESOP-owned in 2001 and transitioned to 100% ESOP ownership in 2013. Hypertherm has made a handful of acquisitions over the past few decades, staying close to its core in manufactured cutting solutions. Acquisitions have been a central component of Hypertherm's growth and value creation, becoming so important that an in-house business development team was created to refine the acquisition strategy and facilitate sourcing, evaluation, and execution of new opportunities. The foundation of this initiative and the acquisition strategy is a combination of the company's deep understanding of industry dynamics, the values rooted in its entrepreneurial culture, and keeping the effects on employees and the ESOP in mind when making decisions.

Before its first ESOP transaction, Hypertherm had established itself as a global manufacturer and marketer of industrial cutting solutions. However, management identified substantial growth opportunities in underserved market segments that could be addressed through a combination of organic innovation and strategic acquisitions (inorganic growth), leveraging strong local market presence and manufacturing capabilities. Inorganic growth through global expansion brought its own complexities, especially in highly regulated industries such as plasma cutting, where regulations can vary from country to country. These stringent requirements made the company think holistically when determining which markets to penetrate, where to sell, what to sell, and how to sell it.

Knowing these core tenets also provided a foundation for understanding which targets to pursue and which to avoid wasting time and resources on. Nearly half of the company's publicly disclosed acquisitions have been completed outside the US, and the most attractive targets had personnel with an understanding of the changing regulatory environment and how those regulations influenced the company's operations. Having an ear close to the ground allows Hypertherm to be more proactive than reactive, and being out in front of the competition has only further solidified its market-leading position. Executive Vice President Sanjeev Srinivasan notes, "The strategic thesis should come first, followed by the investment thesis. We don't acquire for financial engineering purposes; we buy to bring them into the Hypertherm family. Evaluating a target starts with evaluating the needs of our customer base, and the '10-foot radius' of adjacencies where we can fill demand. . . . the key is to identify what products are in demand . . . and whether we can make them ourselves or if we must look to acquire the capabilities from another company."

Another important aspect driving Hypertherm's acquisition strategy is its roots in the culture of the founder. Employee ownership was an extension of the company's founding values, and the organization was aligned to take ownership of problems as they arose and to find ways to solve them. Upholding this culture is of the utmost importance, which is why the company carefully assesses alignment with the target's values before pursuing an acquisition. In 2019, Hypertherm acquired OMAX Corporation, a Washington-based manufacturer of abrasive waterjet systems whose technology and solutions complemented Hypertherm's own offerings. Hypertherm did not need to make any significant changes to OMAX's operations, management structure, or workforce, as its confidence in OMAX's culture and client-first priorities played a significant role in the decision to pursue and complete the acquisition. As an ESOP-owned company, Hypertherm must consider the cultural impacts of an acquisition not only on its own employees but also on those of the target. Integration remains challenging in any situation, but it can be supported by alignment across Hypertherm's workforce and the target's workforce, which enhances their ability to work together and create value.

Evaluating the impact of an acquisition on current employees is further expanded by the global factor that unites international workforces. International employees are often excluded from participating in the ESOP due to complex tax structures and plan administration limits. Through its expansion, Hypertherm has amassed nearly 300 associates outside the US and understands that separating these employees from the ESOP could create a divide in the workforce that negatively affects the company. To address this, Hypertherm developed a compensation package aligned with country-specific employee benefit guidelines to be competitive with the ESOP benefits provided to its US workforce. This strategy reinforces the one-team employee culture.

Hypertherm's acquisitions need to respect the ESOP from a financial perspective as well as culturally, and they require adequate communication to the employee base to be successfully received. Srinivasan states, "Understanding whether the asset is accretive or dilutive is key for an ESOP that is cognizant of its participants, and so targets with EBITDA growing more than 2x top-line revenue growth are more likely to be additive in achieving our long-term growth strategy." Acquisitions can be a very resource-intensive tool for growth, and can affect strategy and shareholder value if done wrong. Even in a target-rich environment, Hypertherm does not pursue every opportunity that comes to its attention, especially acquisitions that would be riskier and could impact its ability to meet ESOP repurchase obligations or severely degrade the annual employee benefit level it can provide. For Hypertherm, a successful acquisition considers all company stakeholders and does not require the company to bet all its chips on synergies being realized immediately. These disciplined acquisitions require a deep understanding of the company's limitations, what additions might be more costly than additive, and what the value creation model is.

Although an acquisition could degrade the company's ability to meet ESOP repurchase obligations, successful acquisitions are also important in driving growth that can fund them. In explaining why Hypertherm chooses to grow inorganically, Srinivasan explains that as the plan matures, "ESOP repurchase obligations begin to rise . . . We know to satisfy the average retirement accounts of 8-10x of employee salaries at exit, we must grow EBITDA faster than we are growing revenue, and so we evaluate targets based on achieving that objective from an inorganic growth perspective."

For all these reasons and more, Hypertherm needed a robust and disciplined acquisition strategy to support its growth. Creating a team with the sole focus of expanding the pipeline was a unique strategy the company employed to not only distribute workflows more evenly and make acquisition processes more efficient, but also because Hypertherm relies on organic searches for opportunities. Targets can truly be anywhere; at conferences, trade shows, and so on, and Hypertherm's most successful acquisitions were those that were sourced through creating relationships with the target company and cultivating those relationships over time. It also gave Hypertherm ample time to sit down with the target's management and truly get a feel for their culture and values, how they operate, and who reports to whom, being mindful of all functions that would need to be integrated post-acquisition. This thoughtfulness has served Hypertherm and its targets well. OMAX co-founder and CEO John Cheung commented, "We wanted a company that would protect our culture, provide stability for our employees, and give our customers products and services consistent with our mission statement." Value creation through acquisitions is realized only through the impact of merging two companies, and Hypertherm's strategy reinforces the fact that it begins with people first.

Jasper Holdings

Corey Rosen

Jasper Holdings is the leading U.S. remanufacturer of power train products. It has more than 4,300 employees and has made several acquisitions. CEO Doug Bawel told the NCEO that Jasper seeks diversification in related industries.[5] For instance, it recently bought a rotational molding company. A critical criterion is culture fit, which Bawel says is more important than strategy. Bawel says they walk through the building and see how managers interact with people and vice versa. They also want to know if the company has peaked. Is there an opportunity for growth because of industry, the right or wrong location, or other factors?

---

5. Doug Bawel, in discussion with the author, May 24, 2024. This and the next three paragraphs are taken from this discussion.

Jasper hired M&A firms to find targets, but that was not successful. Instead, Jasper employees go to conferences looking for companies that may be a fit, including ones that may have an ESOP but need more capital. Additionally, ESOP advisors may have clients who want to be ESOP-owned but decide not to go ahead because of cost or other issues. Jasper has one point person on seeking companies.

Bawel says Jasper Holdings takes a two-pronged approach to its acquisition strategy. "We not only look for companies within the automotive and truck sector but also to diversify outside the automotive and trucking industry. If you're a company with EBITDA in excess of $1 million, you might be a great company to join our ESOP. If an owner has thought about forming its own ESOP, selling to Jasper may be a great alternative for you without the cost of going through the whole ESOP transaction. We like to take the Berkshire Hathaway approach to buying companies that have great leadership and want the opportunity to grow. We don't want to be involved in running the business day-to-day from our holding company. We don't bring our people into the acquired company, but we want to share best practices with the company."

Jasper looks for founders who want to reward their people—it can't get in bidding wars with private equity. It wants companies that have the people to run the company and operate them as standalone companies that can function well on their own.

Finally, Jasper has strong Christian values, and it will buy only companies that are comfortable with that. Its website states, "We will be a good corporate Christian citizen, focused on preserving natural resources, supporting diversity, and giving back to our communities to help them be stronger."[6]

In a video posted by Jasper,[7] several owners and executives from companies that sold to Jasper talk about their experience:

---

6. Jasper Holdings website, accessed July 22, 2024, https://www.jasperholdingsinc.com/.
7. "Jasper Holdings, Inc. - The Acquisition Experience," YouTube, November 30, 2023, https://www.youtube.com/watch?v=utWkvc4a2ic.

- Doug Wayne, former owner of D&W Diesel, said, "We knew the company well. We've done a lot of due diligence together, so I didn't have anxieties or fears, and it's all been played out very well. . . . . They weren't a company to flip and sell the business quickly."
- Jay Miller, president of Diesel USA, said, "All the commitments that were discussed during the time leading up to the due diligence, as well as what followed after the letter of intent, all of the forecasts and promises made, were indeed kept. It didn't surprise me because we have worked with Jasper since the early 60s. I felt I knew the Jasper team very well, a very well-run organization, and they didn't get to where they are today without following through on promises made, so that was not an issue in our minds."
- Terry Strand of Weller Industries said, "There were several examples in our industry of sales that did not go well for owners and senior management, but that was never an issue for Weller. There was definitely fear within our Weller team that major change was going to happen. They were worried they would lose their identity and their leaders, but that fear went away when they realized that it was business as usual. With Jasper, the change to being associate-owned has made a positive impact on our team. Weller already had a great product [and] customer service. The ownership piece, though, helped increase our attention to detail and customer service as owners that really care about the results."
- Paul Weller, former owner of Weller Industries, said, "We found Jasper to be a very good fit because of the ESOP, but more than that because of the Jasper philosophy."

Proponent

Product Expansion and Increased Geographic Footprint

Mary Josephs and Dustin Kim

Proponent is a global aerospace and aircraft parts distribution company with more than 500 employees worldwide. The company set up an ESOP in 1989 and has been 100% employee-owned through an ESOP since 2002. Over the past three decades, Proponent has completed a dozen acquisitions involving companies based in the US and across Europe. Two strategic pillars have driven this activity: expanding its product portfolio and increasing its geographic footprint.

Expanding its product portfolio has allowed Proponent to deepen its specialization and better serve customers across the aerospace supply chain. One of Proponent's earliest acquisition successes occurred in 2003 with Valtec Aircraft Supply, Inc. Valtec, a leading distributor of aircraft sealing and clamp products, broadened Proponent's product specialization and scale. Proponent took a slow and methodical approach to integrating Valtec, a process that spanned several years. Taking a deliberate, measured approach has been a defining pillar of Proponent's acquisition strategy over the past few decades. CEO Andrew Todhunter emphasizes that it is important to be patient when identifying the right acquisition and then complete the integration of the target afterward, to which CFO Steven Frields adds that companies should "not bite off more than you can chew early on" and "maintain a strong sense of humility."

Geographic expansion has been equally central to Proponent's strategy. In a global industry where relationships and responsiveness matter, having a local presence is critical to winning and retaining customers. Establishing operations organically in new markets can be costly and time-consuming, making acquisitions a more efficient path to growth. Proponent has executed on this strategy with disciplined consistency, completing acquisitions involving sites in the UK, France, the Netherlands, Germany, Hong Kong, Singapore, mainland China, and, most recently, Spain. Each transaction has extended the company's geographic footprint while enhancing customer relationships and local market expertise. Proponent's leadership understands that a local presence strengthens sales in international markets, making geographic expansion a cornerstone of the company's long-term growth strategy.

Having completed 12 acquisitions over the past 25 years, Proponent recognizes that networking and intentional relationship building are essential to successful deal-making. Many transactions take years of cultivation before a deal is possible. In the case of Avio-Diepen, a stocking distributor focused on commercial aircraft components for MROs and airlines in the aftermarket, Proponent executives had discussions with the company's leadership for nearly a decade before finalizing a deal. For Proponent's acquisition of HC Pacific, a stocking distributor in the defense sector, the leadership teams of the two companies had known each other for well over ten years. Similarly, with Avioparts, a global leader in aircraft tires, aviation lubricants, chemicals, and logistic solutions, existing relationships and ongoing contact at trade shows helped initiate negotiations. This long-term approach to relationship building has been a defining feature of how Proponent identifies and closes acquisitions that align with its strategic objectives.

Empowered Ventures

Corey Rosen

Empowered Ventures is an Indiana-based 100% ESOP holding company of four companies. Its website states, "We offer business owners a succession plan that leaves their life's work in good hands—the employees. We pay a fair market price while providing peace of mind."[8] Their target criteria include companies where:

- The owner values their legacy and employees.
- An existing team leads the day-to-day operations.
- There is a strong people-oriented culture.[9]

The company should be a B2B manufacturer, distribution, ecommerce, or service provider with outstanding customer service relative to the competition and a differentiated product or service. Target com-

---

8. "About Empowered Ventures," Empowered Ventures, accessed July 18, 2024, https://empowered.ventures/about/.
9. "Our Approach," Empowered Ventures, accessed July 18, 2024, https://empowered.ventures/our-approach/.

panies should have $1–5 million in annual owner earnings, a 10%-plus net profit margin, and a history of steady sales growth and profits.[10]

One of the acquired firms is Firstar Precision Corporation, a Brunswick, Ohio-based precision machining company with 38 employees.[11] David Tenny started Firstar in 2000, and by 2019, he was looking to sell. David had known about ESOPs because his wife worked at Kraft Fluid Industries, a longtime, successful ESOP-owned manufacturer in Ohio. Despite multiple efforts to start an ESOP, Tenny says he found the costs unmanageable.

Operating in the industrial space as well as the booming biomedical field and having experienced significant recent growth, the company was an attractive target. Tenny hired a business broker to help find buyers. The process took considerable time, but by late 2020, more than 20 potential buyers had been lined up. The pool was narrowed to 10 entities, and in early 2021, Zoom calls were set up with all 10. The potential buyers included other manufacturers and private equity firms. The top 3 potential buyers were identified, and each submitted letters of intent. The most attractive offer, it turned out, was from Empowered Ventures. Tenny explains, "The top three letters of intent were similar in value at closing, but the additional earnouts Empowered Ventures offered did make their potential value considerably higher." The sale was structured as an asset sale.

Part of what made Empowered Ventures appealing, Tenny believes, was their philosophy. The Empowered Ventures website says its mission is "to help great businesses continue to thrive. To do that, we support great leaders, and we empower workers as owners and beneficiaries of their efforts." Empowered Ventures adds, "Being 100% employee-owned through an ESOP underlies everything we do and enables fulfilling 'next chapters' for sellers and their employees."

Tenny was a machinist by trade, so it was important to him that "the company culture was a collaborative effort. We have always

10. "Our Approach," Empowered Ventures.

11. The Firstar case study is adapted from "Integrating Two Companies: Firstar Precision Corporation Case Study," National Center for Employee Ownership, May 2023, https://www.nceo.org/article/integrating-two-companies-firstar-precision-corporation-case-study.

worked together to achieve the goals that we agreed were paramount for the long-term success of the company and all the employees." When Firstar was put up for sale, Tenny says, "Our average employee tenure exceeded 12 years, with only 20 years in business." He says the company held regular meetings to discuss company business and address employee concerns. "We never had structured teams, committees, etc., but our employees understood they could always discuss anything with me or other management, and it would be addressed accordingly."

Tenny says the employees never wanted Firstar to be sold but were especially concerned about it being sold to a private equity firm. They knew about people in companies that had been acquired that way, and the experience was not encouraging. This level of trepidation is not unusual, Empowered Ventures says, citing experience suggesting that employees are often unclear about why companies must be sold.

Tenny says that shortly after the buyout, Firstar's culture was similar but showed improvement. "The first year, we made significant efforts to educate the employees about the ESOP, but some of the longer-tenured employees were skeptical, expecting a big (holding company) hammer to drop," Tenny says. Sixteen months in, the mood shifted. "Once we received our first ESOP statements in July, the company culture has gone into overdrive. The current employee base is all in and excited for the future of the company and the Empowered Ventures ESOP."

Empowered Ventures Chief Executive Officer Chris Fredricks and Vice President Spencer Springer arrived in April 2021 to finalize the transaction and formally introduce themselves and Empowered Ventures to the employees. Their approach, however, was largely aimed at supporting the existing management team, Tenny says. "Other than adding a VP of finance (at my request) in June of 2021, they have had very little involvement with the day-to-day operations of Firstar. At the transition, they told me and the management team to continue doing what we have successfully done for the past 20 years."

Tenny calls Empowered Ventures a great resource, especially in helping with improving overall company management. "One (improvement) to mention is establishing a budget," Tenny says. "We never understood the necessity and initially resisted establishing a budget, but after we finalized and implemented our fiscal budget for this year, we have found it to be a great resource, and we refer to it almost daily."

The COVID-19 pandemic negatively affected the company, but Tenny says Firstar rebounded in 2021. "There have been no major changes to our incoming business, as we have been running over capacity since the transition," he says. "At the transition, we had 25 employees. We now have 38 employees and are still looking to fill other openings. I strongly believe that being an ESOP has given us a significant edge over our competitors when it comes to hiring."

As for the so-called Great Resignation? Tenny says only one employee has left voluntarily since the ESOP transition. The ESOP and strengthened culture, plus an enhanced overall benefits package, have made Firstar an employer of choice in the local area.

"The employees of Firstar Precision have hit the lottery with Empowered Ventures," Tenny concludes. "All they have asked from us is to continue doing what we are the best at: making precision-machined components for the manufacturing industry. For me, personally, it has been very gratifying to keep leading Firstar as part of Empowered Ventures. I am so happy that all the Firstar employees are now owners through the Empowered Ventures ESOP. The future is bright for Firstar, and I couldn't be prouder."

Roush Auto Group

Corey Rosen

Roush Honda is a 100% ESOP-owned auto dealer in Westerville, Ohio.[12] It has made one acquisition, Valley Honda in Aurora, Illinois. Bob Navarre, owner of Valley Honda, had been thinking about employee ownership for his business for years. Valley Honda has long had what Navarre calls a "phenomenal" culture. He says that when

12. The Roush Honda case study is adapted from "Another Way to Become Employee-Owned: Selling Your Business to an ESOP Company," *Employee Ownership Report* 41, no 12 (December 2021): 3.

an employee told him, "I love working for you," he would reply, "You don't work for me. No one comes to work for me. We have a common vision, and we're all working for that vision; we're all working for our families." The idea of becoming employee-owned first became concrete for him at his former business, a Toyota dealership, when he noticed how many of their customers were employee-owners at a very successful nearby company. "We had people coming in to buy their cars from us; I noticed all those young people who were really successful." Another spark for Navarre was a company he already knew and loved: Bob's Red Mill. After Bob's Red Mill became employee-owned, Navarre watched the videos on its website about what it means to be employee-owned, and he kept being impressed with the company's accomplishments since its transition.

Navarre knew that a sale to a public company or typical buyer was not the right fit for him or Valley Honda. He believes that maintaining a strong culture "is hard to do in the context of a public company or conglomerate," so he concluded that "from the beginning, ownership by a public company simply wasn't the game plan I wanted." He says the question he kept coming back to was, "Someone will own this business after me. How do we want to set it up so it's good for people who work here?"

An ESOP for his own company seemed like a possible solution. As he started investigating the idea, however, he found that "the more I learned, the more I realized the complexity of setting up an ESOP. I wasn't deterred, but it was clearly going to be a lot of work." Navarre worked hard to learn all he could about ESOPs, and part of his learning process was to reach out to other ESOP companies. He contacted Jeff Brindley, the CEO of a respected ESOP-owned company, Roush Holdings of Columbus, Ohio. Brindley came to Naperville along with Roush's CFO and COO. That visit was the turning point in Navarre's thinking about who should own Valley Honda. A major factor that influenced Navarre's thinking was the care the Roush leadership took with the executives of Valley Honda. "As an entrepreneur, day-to-day leadership is one key thing I was thinking about. We had a fantastic leadership team, and I wanted to know who led our leaders," he said. The Roush leadership team spent several hours with the Valley Honda leaders, talking about operational nuts and bolts and about management philosophy.

Thinking back to that day, Navarre says, "Talking with the Roush leadership was the last piece of the puzzle for me." In this case, Roush also had another advantage—as an automotive dealer itself, Roush would have an easier time with the vital issue of securing the agreement of the manufacturer, without which an ownership transition would be impossible. After the sale was completed, Navarre was invited to join Roush's board. When he took that position, he ended his operational role at Valley Honda. Looking back on the sale, Navarre says, "I feel even better about the sale today than I did on day one. It was the perfect fit for our company." He believes that the combined company—the 240 employees at Valley Honda plus the 300 at Roush Holdings—is bigger and better than the sum of the parts. "We took the culture we had and took it to a whole new level."

CHAPTER 9

Financing Alternatives for ESOPs Pursuing M&A

John Solimine

THE FINANCING LANDSCAPE for ESOPs and employee-owned companies to access growth capital has expanded significantly in recent years. These financing alternatives include a broader menu of traditional debt sources and alternative forms of capital that had previously only supported private equity-owned companies.

Historically, senior debt from a commercial bank in the form of a revolving credit facility or term loan was the only source of financing for ESOPs and employee-owned companies. While commercial banks continue to be the predominant source of financing for both new and existing ESOPs, nonbank lenders, mezzanine debt funds, structured capital, and even minority equity can serve to complement traditional bank borrowing as alternative forms of growth capital.

Commercial Bank Debt: Revolving Credit Facilities or Term Loan

An ESOP company most often partners with its existing commercial bank lender when evaluating an acquisition. Commercial bank financing for acquisitions or strategic growth initiatives can take the form of financing under a revolving credit facility—whether asset-based or a cash flow revolver—or, more typically, under a term loan facility. Such a facility is secured by the company's assets and generally leverages the combined pro forma EBITDA of the existing company and acquisition target. Revolving credit facilities and term loans provided by banks usually have five-year maturities with floating pricing based on the secured overnight financing rate (SOFR) plus an applicable margin reflecting the leverage and risk profile. It is common for banks to tie the pricing to a leverage grid, whereby the margin or pricing on the loan decreases as the company pays down debt.

A company generally collaborates with its existing lender when evaluating a potential acquisition, given its strategic relationship and history with the bank. With its commercial bank, the company often identifies and screens potential acquisition targets from an industry, end-market, or geographic standpoint. An ESOP company should seek to actively maintain a quarterly dialogue with its commercial lender or bank group around strategic growth initiatives, including understanding its debt capacity and how much it could borrow for a potential acquisition. Typically, this represents a leverage threshold or multiple of EBITDA, or the ratio of senior-funded debt/EBITDA. While the financing markets continuously evolve based on economic and macro conditions, the bank financing market remains stable and constructive. After a relatively choppy and cautious lending market, banks have signaled that loan growth is a priority. This has translated into favorable borrower terms on leverage, pricing, covenants, and terms.

The leverage environment largely depends on the size of the company, industry, and credit profile. Generally, senior debt/EBITDA ratios from banks top out in the 2.5x-3.0x range, with a strong underwriting focus on the ability to repay the loan contractually through structured amortization and to demonstrate covenant compliance under different sensitivity analyses. Banks usually focus on a maximum-funded leverage covenant and a minimum fixed-charge ratio as the primary financial covenants. General pricing for a bank facility will depend on the structure and credit profile. For instance, an asset-based facility with full collateral coverage can be priced in the SOFR + 150-250 bps area, while a cash flow loan would be priced around SOFR + 250-350 bps.

As to funding acquisitions beyond these key financing metrics, banks also tend to zero in on pro forma financials, integration, strategic fit, management team, and how the acquisition target would strengthen the borrower. When a company works with a bank, depending on the size of the target, the company can work with its existing lender, expand to a "club" financing with another bank or two joining the financing as participants, or pursue a more broadly syndicated credit facility that tends to include a number of participant banks along with an agent or lead lender.

Nonbank Debt: Term Loan or Unitranche Facilities

The spectrum of nonbank financing alternatives for middle-market companies has expanded dramatically in recent years. Historically, this form of financing, provided by nonbank lenders, credit funds, business development companies, asset managers, and other institutional investors, was reserved for funding larger companies and companies owned by private equity funds.

Today, companies with as little as $50–100 million in annual revenues and $5–10 million in EBITDA can access capital from nonbank lenders as a complement to traditional bank borrowing and as an alternative form of capital for acquisitions. This universe of nonbank capital partners has further entered the ESOP space as a direct financing source for employee-owned companies.

Typically, nonbank financing embodies a term-loan structure or a unitranche credit facility that provides and facilitates funded leverage levels beyond those of a commercial bank. In exchange for this higher level of funded debt or leverage, nonbank credit facilities carry a higher cost of capital than bank facilities and can provide more flexible repayment terms.

Essentially, a unitranche facility is a blended credit facility that combines senior and mezzanine financing, or junior, subordinated debt, into a single credit facility, rather than having separate senior bank and mezzanine debt facilities. As mentioned, these facilities allow for higher leverage levels, typically in the 4.0x-5.5x area, depending on the credit, industry, and overall underwriting. In exchange for this higher financing level at close, nonbank financing can be priced at SOFR+500-600 bps with amortization or required repayment of only 1% per year with a bullet at maturity.

These facilities can also be employed in acquisitions, particularly if the pro forma or combined EBITDA is leveraged under a combined credit facility. This can simplify the financing process compared to a split bank/mezzanine debt structure. It also streamlines the negotiation process by eliminating an intercreditor agreement between the bank and mezzanine fund, working with a single lender, and, in some cases, having an all-in lower cost of capital or loan pricing compared to a bank/mezzanine debt facility.

Mezzanine Debt

Mezzanine debt is a form of subordinated financing that can provide longer-term, incremental capital for M&A or other purposes beyond a company's senior debt capacity. It is a highly flexible form of financing from a structure, rate, and tenure standpoint. Plus, it usually has customizable repayment terms that can be tailored to a company's needs.

Mezzanine debt generally matures in seven-plus years and is priced with a combination of a cash pay coupon and a payment-in-kind (PIK) component. In select instances, it includes warrants to provide incremental return opportunities. The all-in pricing for mezzanine debt is normally in the 12%–14% range, depending on the company size, credit profile, and other underwriting considerations. Mezzanine debt is also flexible from a repayment standpoint because it is typically interest-only for the first couple of years, providing the borrower with repayment flexibility.

From a leverage standpoint, mezzanine debt usually provides capital beyond a senior lender, up to 5.0x–5.5x total leverage. ESOP companies can use mezzanine debt to finance an acquisition when they have limited senior debt capacity or need to reserve their senior debt capacity for corporate operating purposes, such as working capital. Accessing mezzanine debt for an acquisition does not require disrupting a current bank facility or relationship. Rather, it involves bringing in a mezzanine debt fund to provide junior or subordinated capital under more flexible terms in exchange for a higher overall cost of capital.

Mezzanine debt can provide that level of "hard to raise" capital to fund an acquisition instead of having to access equity capital that can prove challenging under an ESOP structure. This financing type also does not dilute the ESOP or other equity holders. Typically, mezzanine debt investors also like to get involved with supporting the company from a strategy and operating standpoint, and they will have board of directors observation rights.

Structured or Minority Equity via Drop-Down LLC

In select transactions, 100% ESOP-owned companies have secured structured equity or minority equity capital to complete a significant acquisition. This more transformative approach, as compared to debt financing alternatives, typically involves restructuring either the ESOP or the company to raise equity capital within the confines of an ESOP structure. Generally, this is achieved through a drop-down LLC structure. It permits an equity investor to provide capital while achieving the benefits of a pass-through structure and avoiding the complexities of subordinated notes, warrant/derivative structures, or second-class-of-stock issues within an S corporation. Within a drop-down LLC structure, the ESOP continues to own 100% of the S corporation, and a new LLC is created below the S corporation.

The LLC becomes the new operating company with the business's assets, customers, contracts, and so on. The benefit of this structure includes the flexibility to establish outside equity for an acquisition, specifically for larger acquisitions where financing through debt alternatives would not be feasible. This maintains the benefits of the 100% ESOP-owned S corporation structure. However, many legal nuances exist, so it is important to thoroughly vet and understand the implications of the required restructuring and related costs in advance with attorneys and other advisors.

ESOPs enjoy more flexibility in raising equity capital under a C corporation structure since no restrictions exist concerning a second class of stock. As long as the ESOP owns the highest and best class of stock and the transaction meets the relative fairness guidelines for ESOPs, equity capital can be raised under a C corporation ESOP structure for an acquisition.

As ESOPs evaluate strategic growth initiatives through M&A, a broad and expanding landscape of potential capital alternatives exists. This menu of capital available to ESOPs is expected to continue to grow, reflecting the breadth of capital available today and the strong interest from lenders and investors in supporting employee-owned companies.

CHAPTER 10

Should You Create a Holding Company?

Daniel Goldstein

What Is a Holding Company?

A holding company is a parent company that buys shares in other companies to hold. For most ESOP companies, the appropriateness of creating a holding company will most likely arise when considering whether to transform from an existing standalone ESOP company to an ESOP-owned holding company. There could be a case for starting a new ESOP-owned holding company from a rollup strategy that combines separate companies into a new holding company portfolio, but this chapter does not address that strategy. This chapter focuses exclusively on ESOP companies that ask themselves whether a holding company structure is right for them.

An existing standalone company will most likely consider the holding company model when deciding whether to make acquisitions or to spin off existing divisions into separate companies, perhaps in combination with a plan to pursue future acquisitions. There are several primary issues to consider when evaluating the standalone versus holding company structure. First, a disclaimer: I am not an attorney or CPA, and you will want to speak with your corporate counsel, your trustee and their valuation partner, and probably several other of your external partners (audit, TPA, culture, and communications) in determining whether to transform to a holding company structure.

Acquisitions and Brand Identity, with a Few Miscellaneous Considerations

There are many strategies for pursuing acquisitions and, consequently, considerations for what to do with the brands post-acquisition.

- Horizontal acquisitions can add territory, buy capacity and competency, remove competitors, and inorganically grow the existing core business. If this strategy is pursued, it would likely make more sense, from a branding perspective, to tuck the acquisitions into the existing company and brand. For example, if Jane's Plumbing Distributor buys mom-and-pop distributors in the surrounding region, it might make sense to rebrand those newly acquired businesses under the Jane's Plumbing Distributor brand. There may, however, still be reasons to establish separate corporate entities for each acquisition, even if branding as a single entity. For example, if Rainy Day Car Wash buys competitors in the region, even if they change each to the Rainy Day Car Wash brand, they still might want each location to be a separate limited liability, C, or S corporation for separation of liability or other reasons specified below.
- Vertical acquisitions can effectively secure supply chain and/or distribution advantages. If the acquisition is intended to remain exclusively proprietary, there may be a good reason to assimilate it into the core company. It could, however, make sense for these acquisitions to continue to exist as independent companies, possibly even supplying competitors or distributing competitors' products or services. In that case, there may be a need to independently brand the acquisition and use a holding company to better separate the businesses. For example, if Penguin Air Conditioning buys its supplier Daffy Duct Works, it needs to decide whether Daffy will produce ducts solely for Penguin or also for independent contractors, distributors, and maybe direct competitors. If Daffy will manufacture ducts only for Penguin, then it might make sense to absorb Daffy into Penguin. If not, there may be a need to preserve Daffy's brand and independence, which may be better accomplished with a holding company.

- Tangentially connected or unrelated business acquisition strategies are much more likely to fit well with a holding company to ensure brand independence. This was the case at Folience, where I was the CEO of this 100% ESOP-owned company. We had legacy newspaper and media businesses, and then we started to diversify by buying an ambulance manufacturing company. It would have made no sense to absorb the ambulance manufacturing business into the media company. The Folience holding company created a platform for acquiring other unrelated businesses, such as when it acquired Cimarron Trailers.

There are liability issues to consider (this is where you seek out your corporate counsel!) when deciding whether to tuck an acquisition into an existing company or keep it as a separate entity. This is true for both stock purchase acquisitions (SPAs) and asset purchases. The SPA can be kept as its own legal entity or undone and absorbed into the acquiree. Assets can be absorbed into the purchasing company, or the purchaser can set up a new separate entity to form a company around the acquired assets. One reason for setting up a new entity for purchased assets could be to take advantage of economic development incentives (in which case you should speak with economic development agencies before making that decision).

Sellers increasingly seek ESOP holding companies as an effective means of transitioning their businesses to employee ownership. Selling to an ESOP is less costly and complex than setting up a new ESOP. The ESOP buyer already has an ESOP plan in place with the necessary trusted partners hired, often with an established employee ownership culture, communication plan, and development in place to help integrate the acquired company, and can almost completely remove the added stress for the acquired company of trying to manage its business while also figuring out how to manage an ESOP. Also, establishing a new ESOP typically requires the seller to finance a substantial portion of the transaction price with seller notes. Selling to an ESOP holding company, in contrast, can often offer the seller a 100% cash deal. There are also operational synergies, addressed below.

If the seller is truly motivated to transition their company to employee ownership, there is no downside to selling to an ESOP unless the seller's ego gets in the way. If the acquired company is folded into a standalone ESOP, there will be an existing hierarchy that most likely places the management of the acquired business under an existing management hierarchy. This may be alleviated somewhat by being acquired by an ESOP holding company, if the portfolio companies retain some measure of autonomy. The largest ESOP holding companies typically acquire large businesses that remain almost fully autonomous after acquisition. Mid-tier ESOP holding companies typically preserve some autonomy at the portfolio company level while supplementing the management with shared services housed in the parent company. ESOP holding companies that acquire small businesses often largely or wholly step in to run the acquired business. In all of these situations, even portfolio companies with presidents and senior leadership teams report to a parent company that has a CEO and a governing board. So long as egos do not get in the way, not only does it work well for sellers to sell to an ESOP holding company, but it also creates new paths for leadership, as portfolio management can take on expanded roles within and across the holding company.

The last issue regarding the acquisition advantages and differences of the holding company is the most complex, so I will only touch on it briefly. The ESOP holding company structure allows for many creative solutions, such as Section 1042 exchange and plan mergers, using drop-down LLCs to carve out ownership and bring in investment capital, and much more. It's a little like going on safari: with the right expert guide looking out for your safety, I recommend the trip, but don't try to go at it on your own!

Administrative Decisions: Complexity and Flexibility

The complexity and flexibility of standalone versus holding company ESOPs can provide challenges and opportunities. Antidiscriminatory practices in benefit administration may mean there is little to no flexibility in tailoring benefits to different pools of employees in a standalone company ESOP, whereas there might be greater flexibility to offer different benefit packages to disparate employee populations of the individual businesses within a holding company. Sometimes, economies of scale tip the scales toward combining all employees under one plan, and other times, each business's employee population is better off continuing under its separate plan. Consult your benefit partners (and TPA, ERISA counsel, and trustee) when determining the advantages and disadvantages of bringing everything together or leaving different plans in place when making acquisitions. This is also true when setting a compensation policy. It is generally easier to structure incentive pay and other compensation policies that are individually tailored to each business in a holding company portfolio than to differentiate policies across departments if the acquired company is absorbed. For example, shift hours, PTO, profit-sharing calculations, and other compensation components can be more easily set with different criteria in diverse portfolio companies.

Similarly, there are business administration issues to consider. How will the valuation or audit be conducted in a standalone company versus a holding company? You also might want to inquire whether the multiple calculated in your share value will be affected. The valuations of companies with lower EBITDA or revenue are usually discounted more than those of larger companies. The sum of valuing eight $50 million revenue portfolio companies may not equal the value of one $400 million revenue company. (Talk to your trustee, to its valuation firm, and to your auditor.) How will debt be considered, and where will it be held? (Talk with your senior lender, and don't forget to consider that subordinated debt might be added in future acquisitions.) You also might want to inquire whether the multiple calculated in your share value will be affected.

How might you be considered under certain affiliation rules? For example, when Iowa distributed American Rescue Plan Act (ARPA) funds to stimulate investment in advanced manufacturing technologies, companies with 76 to 250 employees were eligible. A standalone ESOP company with 500 employees would, therefore, not qualify. However, a separate portfolio company with 200 employees that was part of an ESOP holding company with 500 employees across all its businesses did qualify because there was a carveout for ESOPs that exempted them from the affiliation rules. Sometimes this affiliation carveout applies, as it did for PPP applications and funding, and sometimes it does not apply, as it did not for the Employee Retention Tax Credit application and funding.

Culture and Synergies

It is difficult to put all the considerations for whether an ESOP-owned holding company structure is right for you into one short chapter. A critical consideration is, of course, culture. Building a cohesive culture that spans a single company faces far fewer challenges than building a cohesive culture across a portfolio of companies when each business has its own brand and identity. Imagine an ESOP holding company, NCEO Enterprises, with a portfolio that includes all our fictional examples: Jane's Plumbing Distributor, Rainy Day Car Wash, Penguin Air Conditioning, and Daffy Duct Works. There is only one ESOP, NCEO Enterprises. All the portfolio companies have their own brands, identities, locations, and cultures. Furthermore, each of those companies will have its own business cycle with peaks and troughs, which at various times will add to or drag on share value. Many ESOP holding companies have been successful in developing cultures that provide the glue to unify the employee-owners across a portfolio of companies, even highly uncorrelated companies. In fact, two were recent winners of the Employee-Owned Company of the Year award, and several were runners-up. Many ESOP companies that make multiple acquisitions try to blend an overall corporate culture with enough autonomy at the acquired firms to retain and build their own cultures when the preexisting cultures were working well. But it does take work to develop and sustain that culture across a portfolio of companies (talk with your communications and culture partners about strategies to do so).

There are myriad operational synergies attained when an ESOP holding company acquires a business. Ease of integration, developing an employee ownership culture, and not requiring the newly converted company managers to be ESOP experts have been mentioned. Also, there are often synergies between portfolio companies to share technologies and expertise in functional areas, vendor management and volume pricing, project management and process ideation, and much more, even sharing or trading equipment and personnel. Access to capital is facilitated when borrowing is done at the parent level and backed by the totality of the portfolio businesses, rather than being entirely dependent on a single standalone business. The breadth of advantages and synergies gained by joining an ESOP holding company depends solely on the creativity and willingness of the portfolio companies to collaborate. As always, the people and the culture will make these synergies advantageous to the whole.

It Depends...

The appropriateness of the holding company structure is highly dependent on your goals, strategy, and composition. The ESOP holding company structure is increasingly used as a path for businesses to convert to employee ownership, as a means of consolidation to achieve economies of scale and succession, and as a differentiator to compete with other buyers in the M&A arena. To best evaluate whether transforming from a standalone ESOP to an ESOP holding company is appropriate for you, and if now is the right time for that transformation, please visit with an existing ESOP holding company (most are very collaborative and would be happy to share their experience) and talk with your trusted advisors and external partners.

About the Authors

John Burgess is an attorney and CPA with Jackson Lewis P.C. in Tampa who helps business owners and executives with retirement plans and executive compensation. He is one of Florida's leading experts on ESOPs, which constitute most of his practice. He represents companies in all types of industries in establishing new ESOPs, and after the ESOP is established, he helps those businesses along their journey as an ESOP company, using his experience in representing mature ESOP companies. He also regularly works with both institutional and individual ESOP trustees in ESOP purchase transactions. In addition, he advises employers, from startups to public companies, on other types of qualified retirement plans and executive compensation plans, particularly equity-based compensation programs. John helped to establish the Florida Center for Employee Ownership and is on its board of directors. He has also been the vice president of programming for the Florida chapter of the ESOP Association and the president of the Florida West Coast Employee Benefits Council.

Lynn DuBois is a partner at ESOP Law Group, LLP, where she focuses her practice on all aspects of ESOPs, including the design, implementation, and operation of ESOPs. Her practice includes company, trustee, and shareholder representation in a wide variety of ESOP transactions, including leveraged buyouts, corporate stock repurchases, ownership succession transactions, and corporate reorganizations. Ms. DuBois received her law degree from Stanford Law School, and she has over 25 years of employee benefits and ERISA experience. She is a frequent speaker on ESOP topics for the National Center for Employee Ownership (NCEO), the ESOP Association, and various business organizations. ESOP Law Group, LLP is a boutique law firm serving clients throughout the United States.

Daniel Goldstein is a seasoned executive leader and experienced board member with 30 years of managing and advising employee-owned and family-owned companies. At the end of 2023, Daniel retired as CEO and president of Folience, a 100% ESOP-owned holding company that he and his team founded and built through acquisitions. Daniel then founded and is the CEO of Go ESOP LLC. He serves on ESOP company boards as board chair, audit committee chair, and compensation committee chair, and he works with ESOP executive teams on M&A, strategy, governance, and culture. Daniel's style of leadership and engagement is based on collaborative participation. To continue advocating for employee ownership, Daniel serves on the NCEO's board.

Mary Josephs is a recognized authority on family and private company finance, governance, and ESOPs. She has 30-plus years of experience assisting with 300 ownership transitions for middle-market companies. Before starting Verit Advisors in 2009, she founded LaSalle National Bank's ESOP group and later led Bank of America-Merrill Lynch's ESOP solutions group. Mary was selected as one of the Most Influential Women in Mid-Market M&A by Mergers & Acquisitions magazine in 2017, 2018, 2019, 2020, and 2021. Crain's Chicago Business recognized Mary as a Notable Entrepreneur in 2019, and Private Board Director magazine named Mary a Director to Watch in 2019. Mary has proudly served on the advisory committee on Employee-Owned S Corporations of America for 20 years. She is also a lifetime member of the ESOP Association and a 40-year member of the NCEO.

Dustin Kim is a senior associate at Verit Advisors, where he focuses on ESOP advisory and brings a multidimensional blend of corporate finance expertise, capital market insight, and disciplined transaction execution to clients navigating ownership transitions. At Verit Advisors, he plays a key role in structuring and executing ESOP transactions while also supporting M&A and broader strategic advisory engagements across a range of industries. Dustin's background spans investment banking and portfolio management, giving him a holistic perspective on valuation, capital formation, and long-term stakeholder outcomes. His experience includes advising middle-market companies through both buy-side and sell-side M&A processes, supporting capital raises, and constructing multi-asset portfolios for high-net-worth clients. He is a CFA charterholder and holds an MBA from the University of Chicago Booth School of Business.

William W. Merten is a partner at Krieg DeVault in its Employee Benefits and ESOP practices. He advises corporations, shareholders, directors, ESOP trustees, and various professionals regarding the use of ESOPs and related strategies in a wide variety of transactions, including management buyouts, ownership succession transactions, private equity transactions, going-private transactions, ESOP company sales, and mergers & acquisitions. Bill speaks frequently for various organizations and has served as an executive compensation professor for DePaul University's Masters of Law in Taxation program. He is a fellow of the American College of Employee Benefits Counsel (ACEBC), has authored numerous articles, and has been recognized by leading publications such as Martindale-Hubbell, American Lawyer Media, Super Lawyers, The Legal 500, and Leading Lawyers Network.

Corey Rosen is the NCEO's founder and former executive director and now is its senior staff member. Corey has spoken on various subjects related to employee ownership all over the world with government, business, and union leaders, and he is regularly quoted in leading magazines and newspapers. He has appeared on national television and radio programs and also has authored four books on employee ownership, plus more than 100 articles for various business, academic, and professional publications. He has authored or coauthored several of the NCEO's practical and research publications. He holds a PhD in political science from Cornell University.

John Solimine is a founding member and managing director at Verit Advisors LLC. John leads Verit's debt capital markets efforts and the execution of ESOP and employee ownership transactions that focus on sourcing, structuring, and arranging various forms of debt or equity capital for Verit's clients. John assists Verit's clients in evaluating and analyzing different types of financing alternatives across the ESOP lifecycle. This includes advising both companies with new ESOPs and mature existing ESOP-owned companies on capital alternatives. He has over 25 years of experience in investment banking, private equity, and debt capital markets, particularly with middle-market companies and private equity sponsors in succession and liquidity transactions. John received his BS in business administration from Loyola University Chicago and his MBA in finance, economics, and strategic management from the University of Chicago Booth School of Business.

Carter Wideman is an analyst at Verit Advisors, where he supports senior team members in executing ESOP transactions, M&A advisory, and strategic alternative engagements across a range of industries. At Verit Advisors, he plays a hands-on role in transaction execution while developing broad exposure to the full spectrum of advisory services the firm provides. Carter's career has spanned both investment banking and private equity, giving him a well-rounded foundation in deal execution, financial analysis, and sector-specific diligence. His experience includes supporting M&A transactions at Prairie Capital Advisors, a boutique investment bank, as well as working on active healthcare deals as a summer analyst at BPOC, a Chicago-based private equity firm. He holds a BS in finance with double minors in accounting and economics from DePaul University, where he graduated summa cum laude.

About the NCEO

The National Center for Employee Ownership (NCEO) is a nonprofit organization that has supported the employee ownership community since 1981. Our mission is to help employee ownership thrive. We have thousands of members because we help people make smart decisions about employee ownership, with everything from reliable information on technical issues to helping companies reach the full potential of employee ownership.

We generate original research, facilitate the exchange of best practices at our live and online events, feature the best and most current writing by experts in our publications, and help employee ownership companies build ownership cultures where employees think and act like owners. NCEO members receive the following benefits and more:

- Customizable communication materials
- Live and recorded webinars presented by experts in the field
- Peer networking groups
- Leadership cohorts for CEOs and other leaders
- Resource-rich curated toolkits
- Current news and analysis
- Personalized support for your employee ownership questions
- Sample documents and checklists from trusted sources
- Actionable data from our research team
- Captive insurance group eligibility and other group benefits
- Preferential prices on all paid resources

To join as a member or order publications, visit our website at www.nceo.org. Order this book at www.nceo.org/r/acquisition.

Made in United States
Orlando, FL
04 November 2026

90206050R00083